THE FACE IN
THE WINDOW

American Plays and Players in Australia,
1850–1915

Douglas W. McDermott

Table of Contents

Foreword

WHEN MY FATHER, Dr. Douglas McDermott, passed away in February of 2010, the manuscript of this book was in the hands of the university press that he hoped would publish it. Sadly, we received their decision not to publish the book just a few days later. In the 14 years since, I have worked to try to find another publisher and wrestled with a variety of challenges, from incompatible file formats and questions about copyright to the loss of my mother and my enduring grief at having to do this without either of my parents. The decision to self-publish the manuscript when I was unable to interest an academic publisher was not an easy one, but I believe that it should be available to other scholars, since it represents so many years of research and scholarly study. Dad was an American theatre historian first and foremost, but he made the study of Australian theatre and the intersection of the two the focus of the last years of his life. I had access to two different versions of this book in manuscript, and I have done my best to reconcile them in a way that feels true to my father's vision. Any errors in accomplishing that are mine.

Dad never completed a preface or dedication for this book, but I know that there are certain people he would have wanted to mention. First and always, his wife of more than 50 years, my mother Nelda McDermott. Dad made his first trip to Australia in the summer of 1985, as an external candidate for a university professorship. He wasn't hired, but he loved the country and the people, and he came home determined to go back. He applied for sabbatical, and a couple of years later, they went to Australia for a full year. They found a second home there, and with Mom's help, Dad began the research that became this book. He arranged a reduced teaching schedule at his home university, California State University Stanislaus, and a visiting fellowship at the University of New South Wales, that allowed them to spend as much as half of each of the next ten years in Australia doing research, seeing theatre, and collecting art, (a collection that now resides in the Davis Museum at Wellesley College). In Australia, they made many friends and professional connections, including Richard Fotheringham, then the Executive Dean of the Faculty of Arts at the University of Queensland. He and Professor Tice L. Miller of the University of Nebraska both reviewed this manuscript before Dad's death, and I'm sure he would have wanted to thank them for their input and support.

Dad was always grateful to Oscar Brockett, his dissertation advisor at the University of Iowa and a lifelong friend and supporter, who also passed away in 2010. He also very much appreciated the encouragement and support of his friends and writing colleagues, Dunbar Ogden, University of California, Berkeley, and the late Robert Sarlos, University of California, Davis. I have no doubt that he would want them mentioned here. Jere Wade and the late Joan Steele were also among his supportive colleagues and friends, and they both offered me important emotional support on this project.

From my end, there are others to acknowledge. I could not have completed the work of bringing this book to publication without the support of my partner, Rob

Batchellor, and my friend and self-publishing guru Carolyn Jewel. I also appreciate Jason Baldwin's work on the manuscript and Karen Leuschner-Pearson's work creating the index. Last but never least, I must express my love and gratitude to my siblings Lisa, James, Pamela, Monika, and David, for their trust and patience, and to my "Irish brother" Tony Lynch for his support.

Julia McDermott

Introduction

IN 1973, JAMES MOLLISON, director of the new National Gallery in the Australian capital of Canberra, paid 1.3 million dollars for Jackson Pollack's painting *Blue Poles*. Arousing hostile commentary, the purchase was popularly regarded as the harbinger of events that led the governor general to dismiss the government of Prime Minister Gough Whitlam three years later. The painting, like Whitlam, is now regarded as an icon of Australian culture, an image of the nation's independence and identity (Smee, *Sydney Morning Herald*, 25 January 2001:16). While the facts in this book pertain to theatre in the nineteenth century, it is more about the role American images played in the construction of Australian culture and what that implied about both Australia and America.

The agents of these images were actors. Actors make choices. Given a set of circumstances which are normally created by a playwright and contained in a script, they must choose how to make those circumstances physically and emotionally real to an audience. Volume, inflection, tone of voice, pause, gesture, posture, movement, intention, and motivation are all choices. Moreover, each actor's choices must seem appropriate not only to the given circumstances of the character, but also to the choices made by the other actors for their characters. Even when that is successfully accomplished, actors live with uncertainty and risk. During any performance, accidents can happen on stage, behind the scenes, or in the auditorium, and the actors must adjust, adapt, and improvise to carry on.

Beyond their characters, actors must make other successful choices if they are to make a living from their performances. They must choose plays, roles, and performance styles that will please a paying audience. Thus, just as performers must harmonize their choices with each other, so they must harmonize the ensemble of their choices with the expectations of their audience.

In contriving this meeting of expectations, both performers and audiences must negotiate the overlapping social practices in cultural play at any given moment. They meet within a place, a time, and a scheme of payments for performances that have been designated according to some combination of customs and rules created by the society; to be successful the performance must represent some aspect of the society's cultural mythology in a manner both interesting and acceptable to the audience.

While this must always be so, there are circumstances in which the anticipation and satisfaction of expectation is more difficult than in others. This would certainly seem to be the case for performers from one culture performing for audiences of another, which, in spite of the more or less common language, was the case for American and British actors playing in each other's countries. One need only cite the cultural conflict that focused on the relative merits of William Charles Macready and Edwin Forrest and resulted in the Astor Place riot in 1849. A further set of variables had to be accounted for when British and American actors performed in Australia during the nineteenth century. In both cases, the actors brought with them a cultural mythology that varied in subtle ways from that of their audience. Their success depended on making appropriate adjustments of their mythology so that the audience could derive benefit from it.

Although it reaches consciousness through layers of filtration, the urge to be or feel safe and secure operates in everything from our choice of dress (protective coloration) to our choice of friends (herding with others of our kind). In our choice of entertainment, we seek the affirmation not only of our values, priorities, rules, and institutions, but also the denial of that "other" or those others who seem to threaten us by asserting different values, priorities, rules, and institutions. People tell themselves stories about who they are, where they come from, where they are going, and what distinguishes them from others. These stories transform ideas into nature. They inflect facts so that a particular construction or point of view appears to be the product of inevitable natural forces.[1] Because a culture's mythic "nature" becomes imbedded in its social structures, in the shapes and textures of its material culture, and in the images and structures of its self-expression, it creates a sense of cultural identity.[2]

Cultural identity is problematic because it is hegemonic. At its best, it inspires heroism. At its worst, it justifies slavery or genocide. It often does both at once. It is currently fashionable to disapprove of myth or of any cultural practice or institution which is hegemonic. Such disapproval is based on the belief that neither a class nor an individual should have the power to coerce another. Because hegemony is seen as a coercive exercise of power, it is condemned as oppressive. Recent history provides numerous examples of ruling elites using myths of cultural identity to coerce and oppress. Yet oppression is not the inevitable result of hegemony. While cultural conformity may seem to be a conspiracy of the ruling class, it can be, and often is, simply the basis of the laws and customs to which people agree in order to live together in what John Locke called "civil society."

In any event, hegemony seems inevitable. Birth compels the individual to distinguish between self and other; survival compels individuals to identify apparently harmful others. Thus, every culture is driven by both reproductive and evolutionary biology to define itself, at least in part, in terms of who or what it is not. At any moment, there is at the center of a culture a group that asserts its hegemony and strives constantly to extend, enhance, and stabilize it. At varying distances from the center, there are other groups either negotiating for some kind of autonomy or working to encompass the overthrow of the group in the center.

I would suggest that the majority of groups in a society aspire to the values of the dominant one, and that such agreement on values creates a market for cultural expression of those values.[3] People seek affirmation in their beliefs and will patronize those who provide it. Since the dominant group in any society has both a greater vested interest in maintaining cultural stability and a greater power to patronize, it is not surprising that its views should be relatively conservative and disproportionately represented.

However, one should not confuse hegemony with determinism.[4] Apparently hegemonic institutions and practices are more fluid and more varied than generally supposed. As populations increase, essential resources disappear, climates alter, new diseases appear, and new technologies develop, myths are revised in an attempt to preserve the basis of agreement in civil society.

Nineteenth-century theatrical performance offers an example of the variability and fluidity of cultural hegemony. The traditional elite repertory was comprised of tragedy and "genteel" comedy. Shakespeare's plays were the core of this repertory, to which were added historical costume dramas and manners comedies written in the first half of the century. Although it represented the values, manners, institutions, and customs that supported the aristocratic hierarchy, this repertory appealed to all classes, and theatres provided appropriately priced seats for each of them. The appeals of such plays to the working class were multiple. To begin with, there was the appeal of voyeurism. In the theatre, the working class could get a look at the life of the upper classes often denied them outside the theatre. To be sure, it was the view that the elite wanted the working class to have, but one suspects the working class took that into account.

However, Shakespeare's plays contain working class characters and scenes. While on their surface such scenes depict the working class as foolish, at a deeper level they unleash the anarchic, subversive energy of farce that subverts the power of the ruling class. These characters have their own appeal and normally have positive plot functions in the plays. Finally, even when there are no such scenes in these plays, they would be followed in performance by an afterpiece which was usually a farce or musical burlesque—once again releasing those subversive or marginalized elements.

A second, popular repertory competed with the elite one. At its heart were domestic and sensation melodrama. These plays appealed primarily to a non-elite audience because characters representing marginalized social classes nearly always triumphed over representatives of the elite, and where they did not (as in *Camille*) certain elite core values were questioned.

In such a context, one marks the presence of American actors and American plays on the Australian stage. It is easy enough to understand why the actors would come. In America, as in Great Britain, only a few cities were large enough to support resident theatres, so only a few actors could stay in one place for an entire season. Most of them travelled from city to city, town to town, region to region, in search of audiences. Australia was simply another provincial circuit, though farther away. What is less obvious, and therefore more interesting, is why Australian audiences consumed American plays and players. What was it in those representations that resonated with the emerging Australian cultural identity, and what can one infer from those resonances?

The subject of this book is the representation of America on the Australian stage. While Australia's roots are British, many of its historical and geographical realities more closely resembled those of the United States. By looking at the Australian reception of representations of America, I have tried "to take myth seriously on its own terms, and to respect its coherence and complexity, without becoming morally blinded by its poetic power...or else rendering the subject 'safe' by the usual eviscerations of Western empirical analysis."[5]

The result is like looking at a landscape through a window and seeing one's own image reflected in the glass. Just as contemporary Australians see *Blue Poles* as an image of their landscape and identity, so their ancestors saw images of America as examples of things to be either shunned or embraced. There are other things I could have seen and other ways I could have seen them. As Isaiah Berlin pointed out, there are many possible patterns in history and inevitably some patterns appeal more than others (Berlin, 70). My rationale is precisely the appeal of these patterns, which is to say my fascination with the Australian uses of the reflections of American culture I think I see in the window.

The pattern I see seems to have gone through three phases. Until about 1880, Australians thought of themselves as provincial British, and, therefore, "American" meant "not British" in a generally pejorative way. The 1880s was a transition during which the colonists began to think of themselves as "Australians," that is, not exactly "British." In this context, "American" could be a term of praise. Finally, from about 1890 on, Australians once again thought of themselves as "British," but in a different sense than before. They now thought of themselves as "British" in the sense of an independent, self-governing people who were voluntarily part of the British Empire. Insofar as they thought the Empire was in decline, they found that which they called "American," a possible source of reinvigoration. In each phase, performance representations of that which was seen as "American" played a significant role.

Everyone who has written about the history of the theatre in Australia acknowledges the presence of American plays and players. They are seen as minor events in an overwhelmingly British context, and their successes are usually attributed to the triumph of talent over cultural deficiency. One or another specific instance may be singled out because it illustrates a point the historian wants to make. Such an approach is adequate if one considers only one case at a time, but when one looks at the larger picture, most of the major plays and players between 1850 and 1915, anomalies arise: in some cases, those who succeeded in pleasing the Australian press and public do not seem to have been significantly more talented than those who failed; and in some cases, their Australian success far exceeded anything they experienced in the United States. This study is an attempt to explore the possible reasons for these anomalies.

I have limited myself to the period between 1853 and 1915. The beginning is natural. The first American players to be identified as such in Australia were James Stark and his wife, Sarah Kirby, in 1853. The ending may seem arbitrary. I could have stopped with federation in 1901, the chronological close of the nineteenth century; but, as most students of European culture agree, the turn of the century made no difference. The First World War did. In this sense,

Australia's nineteenth century lasted until the end of 1915. By then, Australia and New Zealand had been initiated into the twentieth century by the ritual of Gallipoli. By Boxing Day (26 December), the traditional beginning of a new theatrical season, Australia's daily papers were covered with pictures and accounts of ANZAC casualties.

However, this is not an encyclopedia. I have limited myself to actors in plays. I have omitted the scores of American variety performers who appeared in Australia's theatres and halls. Thus, I take no account of W. C. Fields or Mark Twain, each an icon of idiomatic Americana. In order to render even this data manageable, I have limited myself in two further ways. First, I have only searched the daily newspapers of the six territorial capitals (Adelaide, Brisbane, Hobart, Melbourne, Perth, Sydney). Second, I have featured those performances that seemed to be identified as culturally American.

I have organized the material in two ways. First, there seems to be a change over time. Up to about 1880 most Australians thought of themselves as living in an accidentally displaced home county of England. However, during that decade, voices articulated a unique Australian identity within the context of English-speaking culture. It proved to be the start of the change that led to federation in 1901. I have divided the book accordingly. Throughout the entire period, however, the theatrical repertory remained divided into fairly fixed categories. Leading actors tended to specialize either in the classical repertory, with the plays of Shakespeare at its center, or in the repertory of contemporary melodramatic and comic drama. There were exceptions, of course, and I have dealt with those as separate cases. I have also chosen to feature some stars more than others, and I have included one or two minor players as well. In every case my choice has been guided by my intention to illustrate the interaction of the evolving myths of American and Australian cultures.

CHAPTER 1

The Audience: Australia, 1853

Social Context

IN THE MIDDLE of the nineteenth century, most residents of Great Britain's Australian colonies wanted to be thought of as residents of a geographically displaced English home county. Between 1850 and 1880, they achieved this goal. An understanding of the American influence on the Australian stage, therefore, must begin with some consideration of both the social and the theatrical context in which Victorian Australians lived. To them, the United States of America was a distant land, populated by foreigners with whom they had little contact, but about whom they read a great deal in books like those by Mrs. Trollope and Mr. Dickens.[1]

The colonizing of Australia was controversial. Mocked by some as the realization of a Swiftian satire (a utopia of thieves), advocated by others as part of a rational solution to Britain's burgeoning social unrest, it was intended, like all colonies, to be self-supporting. The experiment was a result of various pressures on Great Britain. The industrial revolution created a growing demand for both cheap raw materials and secure markets for the sale of finished goods. Colonies were a way of satisfying these demands. Historically, colonies had always used cheap slave labor, but those members of the middle class who lived by industrial commerce were primarily evangelical Protestants who increasingly opposed slavery. The loss of most of the North American colonies meant that thousands of felons were imprisoned at home each year rather than transported as indentured labor. The obvious solution was to found a new colony in which convicts could be used as cheap labor.

Australia was a series of experiments in colonization. New South Wales (including the areas later separated as Tasmania and Queensland) was based on convict labor. Western Australia began as a non-convict settlement that later accepted convicts after transportation had ceased in New South Wales. Victoria and South Australia never accepted convicts. That a mixture of criminals, partisans of Irish home rule, discharged military men, yeoman farmers, and tradesmen could triumph over a harsh land of perennial drought, backwards seasons, hostile native inhabitants, and bizarre plants and animals was a source of no little local pride.

By 1851, Australia was a group of self-governing colonies that wished to remain separate from each other. There were 437,665 persons of European descent living in them. Only 1.5 percent of the population were still convicts, while another 14 percent were emancipationists (freed convicts). The majority of people were either born there ("currency lads and lasses") or were free immigrants ("new chums").[2]

Nevertheless, they were often damned with such faint praise as the young Charles Darwin had for them. Distressed by the factionalism, the pursuit of money, and the degrading effect of convict servants, his reaction to Sydney in 1836 was, "To congratulate myself that I was born an Englishman." Although he acknowledged that economic opportunity abounded and that the necessities of life were plentiful and cheap, he concluded, "nothing but rather sharp necessity should compel me to emigrate."[3]

The dissonance between pride in their accomplishments and shame at British reaction to them caused two mutually exclusive views of themselves to flourish among the colonists. One was of Australia as Hell. It began as a prison and most of the first Australians were convicts. The miners of the Australian gold rush and the bushrangers of the outback frontier seemed to confirm convict values. In the masculine society of the convicts, the primary value was equality. All were equal in their own eyes. The second value was loyalty (mateship). Since all were equal, all were obligated to help one another. Finally, the convicts valued the subversion of authority. Any act of disregard or disrespect toward their masters was understood as an act of rebellion, an act that created a space of freedom, however liminal. The local term for such action was "larrikinism," and the perpetrator was called a "larrikin." Gradually, mateship and larrikinism became the basis for Australian popular culture.[4]

The alternative view of Australia as Paradise was espoused by successful free settlers in New South Wales and was widely shared in Victoria and South Australia, which had never received any convicts. They were regional Englishmen and women, not foreign colonials. Great Britain was the source of almost all immigration and investment capital, and it was the primary market for Australian goods. In fact, these would-be provincials were as completely controlled by British economics and culture as the convicts had been by their jailers. Thus, in 1850, even the most loyal British Australians understood egalitarianism, mateship, and mistrust of authority.[5]

In all other ways, they reproduced Victorian culture. Although it was a culture with an established aristocracy, it was increasingly dominated by the money and values espoused by the middle class. By 1850, a high-middle-class culture had emerged, in which those prosperous in the professions and in trade had appropriated what they understood to be the values of the aristocracy, redefining class as economic rather than as hereditary.[6]

The middle class was the beneficiary of a process of change that had its roots in the Middle Ages. Modest improvements in diet and sanitation resulted in better health and longer life. These, in turn, created new attitudes that encouraged education, scientific research, and technical innovation. To accommodate these changes, societies unified and codified everything from weights and measures to laws. The resulting cultural stability stimulated business, investment, and the extension of credit. In the nineteenth century, the application of steam and electricity to transport and communication, combined with the enormous increase in the supply of wealth created by the California and Australia gold rushes, resulted in the creation of whole new forms of business and kinds of industry.

These changes did not occur in an orderly fashion. They happened at different times and rates in the different countries, Great Britain (and later the United States) generally being first. However, these changes did happen in all European countries except Russia, and the experience of the emergent middle class was one of continuous expansion within a framework of carefully codified law, science and custom, and its chief preoccupations were "to ensure the future of one's children, to arrange advantageous marriages and uphold religion and self-control."[7]

The middle class thought of the family as the basic social institution. In an age of rapid economic and social change, a sentimental domestic ethos was intended to secure stability and prosperity. The family was the counterbalance to industrialization and urbanization. It provided a place of familiarity in a world of strangers. The father was the proprietor, the wife the manager, and the children apprentices. The home was its setting. It was the domain of the woman, whose domesticity was her chief virtue, and within which children learned the virtues of discipline and industry that were the basis of success (happiness) and from which males went forth to do battle in business and politics (Ruskin, Lang, Cott, Stickney).[8]

America (the United States) was a free element in the Australian part of this universe; its influence could turn Hell into Paradise, or the opposite. Prior to mid-century, there had been little contact between Australians and Americans. Although an American ship had visited Sydney in 1792, the East India Company monopoly and the British Navigation Acts had kept Australian ports legally closed to all but British ships.[9]

Long before significant contact between the two cultures, British Australians inherited clear stereotypes of America from the writings of British travelers and novelists. Early visitors were most often concerned with America as a suitable place for business or emigration. Many, such as Henry Wansey (1794), Henry Bradshaw Fearon (1817), and William J. Cobbitt (1818) found the country prosperous, the standard of living high, and the mode of society and government satisfactory and appropriate. There was, however, a general condemnation of violence and slavery in otherwise favorable accounts, such as that of Harriett Martineau (1838–1839).

Unquestionably, however, the two most widely read accounts were those of Frances Trollope and Charles Dickens. Mrs. Trollope was perhaps the traveler least pleased with what she experienced. Her view represented those of other British Tories, who viewed the existence of the United States as a threat to their culture because it did away with both the aristocracy and the church as governing institutions. A resident for four years (1828–1831), she visited New Orleans, Memphis, Baltimore, Washington, D. C., and Philadelphia, and resided for nearly two years in and near Cincinnati. Everywhere she found the scenery unpleasant (either dull or terrifying), the climate unhealthy, the people mannerless and humorless, both their idiom and accent painful to her ears. Above all, she found Americans hypocritical. While railing against European tyranny and extolling American liberty, they exiled Indians and enslaved African-Americans.[10]

Dickens's view of America perpetuated an ambivalence first voiced by de Tocqueville. The people were splendid, but there were elements in the society that prevented the development of their best qualities. Americans:

> Are by nature frank, brave, cordial, hospitable, and affectionate. Cultivation and refinement seem but to enhance their warmth of heart and ardent enthusiasm; and it is the possession of these latter qualities in a most remarkable degree, which renders an educated American one of the most endearing and most generous of friends. ...These qualities...are, however, sadly sapped and blighted in their growth among the mass.[11]

Even this view seems generous compared to the American adventures of Martin Chuzzlewit, whose sudden decision to go to America causes his friends much concern. His experiences are nearly all terrible. From the moment he lands in New York, he is assailed by sensationalism, hypocrisy, greed, violence, and filth. He is forced to conclude that for Americans, "He was their champion who, in the brutal fury of his own pursuit, could cast no stigma upon them for the hot knavery of theirs" (273).[12] He witnesses the horror of slavery and racial bigotry (which Dickens thought was the root of American violence), and his experience of the frontier community of Eden is one of unrelieved ugliness and disease. His "great prospects for doing well there" turn out to be a wicked joke, and only the charity of an American allows him to return to the heaven of England.[13]

Australians, however, had access to the writings of Jefferson, Franklin, and Emerson and were capable of contrasting Dickens's view of frontier America with that of Fenimore Cooper. In the world of the latter, the British are invariably wrong. Every aspect of their culture, from their clothes to the values of an aristocratic class system, causes them to suffer in North America. The virtuous are only rescued by the intervention of Natty Bumppo and his neighbors. Although of British stock, these settlers have been born in the new world and have transformed their heritage into a culture that suits the new environment. They can be as socially decent and gentle as the British, but they can be as fierce and wily as the native people. It is, in fact, this combination of new and old world that Cooper presents as the model for his American readers to emulate. Many in Australia hoped for a similar adaptive triumph in their new world. As the *Sydney Colonist* observed in 1837:

> It is natural that Australia should look upon the United States with more than ordinary interest. Throughout the whole of their history, there are certain broad features bearing no imaginary resemblance to our own. …America at length outgrew the trammels of national juvenility, and asserted the prerogatives of matured manhood, which she in the end compelled her reluctant parent to acknowledge: it is perfectly consistent with loyalty and with common sense to predict, that at some future period, far distant no doubt it is, Australia will pursue a similar course, and with similar success.[14]

The events that provided the basis for a direct Australian experience of America were the California and Victorian gold rushes and the American Civil War. During the California gold rush, some six thousand men from New South Wales and Van Diemen's Land (Tasmania) ignored the advice of their governments and emigrated in search of instant wealth. Their experiences were not all positive. To begin with, they were stereotyped as convicts, and the stereotype was reinforced by the criminal activities of the San Francisco gang (mostly from Tasmania) known as the "Sydney Ducks." Moreover, San Francisco's Committee of Vigilance caused concern in Australia. Not only was it an example of America's lawless violence in disregard of legal authority, but Australians were unjustly convicted and two were lynched.[15]

Thus, when the Australian gold rush began in 1853, authorities feared the arrival of Americans. The fears were long-standing. Gold had been discovered in New South Wales in 1841, but officials had hushed it up because they feared the upheaval of a sudden increase in immigration. It was only economic need in 1853 that compelled them to publicize the gold strikes in New South Wales and Victoria. Since placer mining was rapidly failing in California, reverse migration resulted. The Australian miners ("returned Californians") came first, followed by others. Port officials kept no records of immigrants' origins, so it is impossible to say how many Americans participated in the Australian rushes. Estimates range from five to fifteen thousand.

The richest and most numerous finds were in Victoria in the areas of Ballarat and Bendigo, so it was there that most Americans went. Some certainly participated in the Eureka uprising of 1854, and a generalized American influence was blamed for that event. At the same time, however, American miners were respected for their technical knowledge, hard work and ability to cooperate in working a claim. An American, Freeman Cobb, designed and managed the coaches that connected the mining camps with each other, and America provided 40 percent of Victoria's imports. Moreover, reports by gold field officials invariably praised the Americans for being peaceable and law-abiding.[16]

The American Civil War also polarized Australian thinking about the United States. Like all good Britons,

Australians disapproved of slavery. Consequently, there was support for the Union in the belief that it would end that evil in the United States. However, both economic and political self-interest created considerable sympathy for the Confederacy. Australian wool growers were hurt by the war's disruption of the British spinning and weaving industry, and many colonists compared the Confederacy's desire for self-government with their own.

Public support for the Confederacy is most clearly demonstrated by the Shenandoah incident. The Confederate raider Shenandoah docked at a privately leased slip at Port Melbourne on 25 January 1865. In compliance with the Queen's declaration of neutrality in the war, the Victorian government recognized it as an agent of a belligerent power and permitted it to obtain supplies and repairs to its engines. The captain and his officers were fêted at a banquet held in the prestigious Melbourne Club, which was attended by both influential citizens and government officials. In spite of the protest of the American Counsel, and in violation of the neutrality act, its captain also recruited as many as seventy British citizens to serve in the crew before he was permitted to sail on 18 February.[17]

Theatrical Context

In addition to these general cultural attitudes and opinions, Australians came to a theatrical performance with a set of expectations about both plays and performance. If the middle-class parlor was the center of family life, it was also the primary place in which the drama of genteel virtue was enacted through a code of manners that stressed physical and emotional restraint in social visits and entertainments such as musical recitals, charades, and reading aloud. Consequently, when the family went out it regarded the theatre as an extension of that parlor, similar in its furnishings, occupants, and entertainment. Both in performance and in person, the successful actor had to seem acceptable as a guest in that parlor.[18]

The standard repertory was comprised of plays whose stories supported these values with both positive and negative examples. It is sometimes referred to as an "elite" repertory as opposed to a "popular" one because it drew a significant share of its audience from the elite or respectable social classes, though it also drew from the others as well. By contrast, the popular repertory did not draw significantly from the middle and upper classes.

The standard repertory had certain plays by Shakespeare at its core. *Hamlet, Romeo and Juliet, Othello, Macbeth, The Merchant of Venice, As You Like It, Much Ado About Nothing,* and even *Richard III* were regarded as domestic rather than as dynastic. From the point of view of the Victorian audience, they were stories about the success or failure of characters in living up to the values of sentimental domesticity. The politics of royal succession and rebellion, of such vital interest to the original audience, were less pressing for the Victorian British, secure in the persons and institutions of their constitutional monarchy.

The modern plays that formed the rest of this repertory were more obviously related to bourgeois values. Several of those will be described in the discussion of the American actors who most often played them and will illustrate the nexus of values that dominated the Victorian stage. Their stories feature social stability threatened by improper domestic behavior, the family representing all of society. Stability is always restored by means of a character's conversion to or sacrifice for domestic virtue.[19] It was these values that American players had to represent convincingly for the Anglo-Australian audience. They were values deeply rooted in Victorian culture and required an appropriate acting style. They are representative of the expectations that American players had to satisfy.

This repertory was culturally homogenous and accurately represented the dominance of British theatrical practice. The same could be said of the style of acting. While many factors contribute to acting style, all combine in the actor's voice and body, habits of speech and movement. Michael Booth suggests that in this period actors can be divided into two groups: those who played situationally, exploiting each scene, each situation, for maximum effect without undue regard for consistency; and those who played holistically, sacrificing some effects for the sake of an overall coherence of character.[20] While this is certainly true, it is possible to be somewhat more specific by describing actors' performances in terms of persona and absorption.

All actors have strengths and weaknesses. They are limited by the physical and mental attributes with which they are born. Consequently, there are some performance tasks that they do easily, while there are others with which they struggle. This leads them to roles in which they can emphasize their strengths and minimize their weaknesses. This process of adapting their natural abilities to certain roles creates the persona (performance personality). All successful actors do this. The star or featured actor is one who constructs a persona that also represents values popular with the audience. However, the more successful an actor is at doing this, the more he or she is apt to be confined to that persona ad nauseam. For an actor of few resources, such popularity is welcome. For one with abundant resources, it can become a curse. Many popular performers partially escape their stereotypical persona by offering a second one, usually an opposite of the first.

Just as actors vary in their personas, they vary in the degree to which they absorb the audience into their character and its situation. Some actors seem reflective rather than absorptive. They awe or astonish the audience with the technical virtuosity of their performance. The spectator is expected to step back and gaze in awe as at any other natural phenomenon, such as the Grand Canyon or Niagara Falls. At the opposite extreme, some actors seem to invite the spectator to enter into the interior life of the character. The performance absorbs the spectator as Diderot felt absorbed by certain paintings. The greatest stars seem to occupy a position mid-way between the two extremes. They seem to be able to both dazzle and absorb their audience at the same time.[21]

The degree of absorption or reflection in an actor's style can usually be estimated from descriptions of speech and movement. Reflective actors tend to emphasize the sound of the language over its sense. Some actors seem to sing or chant the dialogue rather than speak it. Descriptions of movement also suggest reflection or absorption. Reflective actors' physical performances consisted of carefully choreographed gestures, movements, and poses intended to illustrate almost pantomimically the emotion of the character.

Actors' performances can exhibit any combination of qualities of persona and absorption. However, during the nineteenth century, any actor who exhibited either a single strongly fixed persona or was highly formal in speech or movement was apt to be characterized as artificial and old-fashioned, while one who exhibited some variety of persona or flexibility of voice and movement was apt to be characterized as lifelike and modern. Over the period of time covered by this study, there was a significant shift in audience preference from the formal toward the informal.[22]

An illustration of this tendency can be found in Fred Myrtle's review of *Othello* at the Columbia Theatre, San Francisco, published in *The Dramatic Mirror* of 4 March

1899. The actors—Louis James, Frederick Warde, and Kathryn Kidder—were popular provincial stars, whose status in the American theatrical hierarchy of the day was just below the first rank occupied by Edwin Booth (still alive in everyone's memory), Joseph Jefferson, James O'Neill, John Drew, and Ada Rehan:

> The Othello of Mr. James and the Iago of Mr. Warde have been seen often by San Francisco playgoers, but it was the consensus of opinion that neither had been seen to such advantage before. Mr. James was more serious and expressive in his interpretation of the character. Mr. Warde showed a marked improvement in his style; he was less demonstrative and more flexible. Miss Kidder, as Desdemona, showed what a really clever actress she is. Not deep or passionate enough, perhaps, to please most readers of Shakespeare, but always dignified and self-controlled. She is quite classical in style and her speaking of the lines charmed all.

From this description, one can infer that in response to shifting audience taste, James and Warde were moving further toward an absorptive style that was "expressive" and "more flexible," while Kidder remained firmly based on an older style that, while not quite fashionable, was still perfectly acceptable. The critic (and presumably the audience) had no problem with actors of different styles playing together in the same performance.

Nor was there anything like a steady movement from one extreme to another over a period of time. It would seem that Warde had shifted more than James. However, actors at both extremes competed successfully with each other (often in the same performance, as Warde and Kidder did here) for audience favor during the entire period. Moreover, it seems clear that provincial audiences tended to prefer an older style. The stylistic shift in E. H. Sothern's

Hamlet indicates this. When he first played the role in New York City, the *Dramatic Mirror's* critic thought that while in many ways it was traditional and inconsistent, it was "human" (29 September 1900:16), but after three seasons of touring, the reviewer thought, "He is now a more melodramatic Hamlet. He seems to have adopted, to an extent, the methods of some of the old school tragedians, who sacrificed all to strength and power. He is much more vociferous, much less appealing than before" (10 January 1903:16-17). In short, he had adapted his style of playing to the dominant taste of the provincial audience.

The established style of acting at the mid-point of the nineteenth century was a composite of influences, but it tended to favor strong single personas and a relatively high degree of reflection. In the background was the style of the Kemble family, which emphasized a fixed persona, round tones and regular meter in the speaking of verse, and aristocratic posture and gesture in action. As a consequence, it was more astonishing than absorptive. It had been modified by Edmund Kean and Junius Brutus Booth, who had introduced violent stage action while retaining the Kemble voice and speech patterns. This change presented what seemed like different personas in different roles, and thus, while still awe-inspiring, their acting was seen as more life-like.

The style was revolutionized by William Charles Macready, who retained the Kemble voice while breaking the verse meter to achieve a more "natural" effect, and who disciplined the excesses of Kean's and Booth's physical action. Macready also extended the tragic repertory to include selected modern plays. The effect was one of significantly greater flexibility and absorptiveness.

Generally speaking, stylistic changes were first supported in the major cities. Provincial audiences were conservative in their taste. This was especially true in terms of speech. Proper pronunciation and careful diction were hallmarks of the middle class. Consequently, provincial audiences often preferred a style like that of the Kembles, distinguished by graceful gestures, careful diction, and round tones. Something of the general identification of proper speaking with acting is suggested by the following comment about an American actress appearing in a modern play in San Francisco, "In the first part of the play the language falling to the heroine is so nearly conventional that she has not much chance to show her qualities in declamation or as an actress" (*Alta*, 6 August 1872).

Moreover, as Beverley Kingston has suggested, the speech of the nineteenth century Australian worker, "was probably a little less broad than is usual today, though it may have been slower, more deliberate, more self-consciously correct than that of his English-born counter-parts. ...Among educated Australians...a recognizable form of educated English was heard."[23] Correct speech was part of proper manners. Actors had to speak in a fashion that was believed to be appropriate, and, in the case of Shakespeare, appropriate for verse. As George Vandenhoff said in his popular *Art of Elocution*:

> Poetry is a more exalted style of composition than prose: and the Elocution must keep pace with the subject or matter. The voice must flow more softly; must undulate gently, and not jump or jerk on the inflections; so that the verse may run smoothly and without jar upon the ear.[24]

English visitors to America regularly commented on the uncouth pronunciation of the locals. Captain Frederick Marryat observed, "They appear to have no exact rule to guide them...the accent being generally laid on the wrong syllable. In fact, everyone appears to be independent, and pronounces just as he pleases" (183–184).[25] Americans accent more syllables, and do so more heavily, than

Australians, even today, and the more frequent, heavier emphasis tends to produce elongated, drawling vowels. This is particularly noticeable in blank verse. Compared to Anglo-Australian use, American seems to plod or drag. That is possibly what the critic James Smith was referring to when he criticized James Stark's reading of verse, "He lays the same stress upon minor and insignificant passages, and brings them into the same prominence as he does those of a more weighty, passionate and masterful character" (*Argus*, 21 June 1856).

While American actors such as Edwin Forrest and Charlotte Cushman had developed a style of playing based on the examples of Edmund Kean and Junius Brutus Booth, the United States supported a universe of successful provincial actors who developed individual approaches popular with regional audiences. Thus, although New York City was the capital of American theatricals, there was a much greater provincial independence than in England or Australia. The result was a range of styles as large and expansive as the nation itself, not only vocally and physically more exaggerated than its British counterpart, but also favoring individuality of interpretation in line reading and stage business. It was a style that inclined more to fixed persona and awe than to flexibility and absorption.

Thus, when American actors appeared on the Australian colonial stage, they inserted themselves into a context of competing ideas about personal and national identity, and their performances became representations of another culture that were viewed as either appropriate or not. The challenge for visiting performers was to find places where they fit, places where their representations of America functioned harmoniously with the audience's ideas about both Australia and America (Fotheringham).

This process was complex. If American actors simply fit into the traditions of content and style accepted by the audience, they would have caused no notice as Americans. That seems to have been the case with Maria Watkins Burroughs (the first wife of George Coppin), Mrs. Charles Poole, and Daniel Waller. Those who didn't fit at all, who were simply novel in their approach, like McKean Buchanan, Jane Coombs, or Katie Putnam, failed. Successful American actors fit, but they contributed something new in the process. As T. S. Eliot points out:

> The existing order is complete before the new work arrives; for order to persist after the supervention of novelty, the whole existing order must be, if ever so slightly, altered; and so the relations, proportions, values of each work of art toward the whole are readjusted.[26]

Let me suggest a general theory of how that happened for American plays and players in Australia. By the middle of the nineteenth century, European culture had completed a tectonic shift from the feudal system to the market system. In the former, a small hereditary aristocracy owned the primary means of production (land) and assumed the obligation to provide for the welfare of everyone else. In the latter, the means of production were more varied, including tools, machines, and agencies for the transfer of wealth (shops, banks), and ownership was more fluid. The means of production were regularly bought and sold without regard for heredity or class.

In this shift, Great Britain was slower than the United States because it retained its aristocracy and their privileges. By contrast, America had no aristocracy except wealth, and almost anyone, it seemed, regardless of birth, could amass wealth by means of hard work, thrift, and shrewd dealing. Australia was somewhere between. While wholly British in its cultural heritage, it had no pre-existing aristocracy of its own and so allowed for greater social and economic mobility than the home country.

To the extent that Australia was more middle-class and market-driven, it seemed to like the more absorptive and understated American style of writing and acting better than the British did. It may be that the older, more heroic reflective style was associated with cultural notions of aristocratic responsibility and leadership and seemed more appropriate in Great Britain, while the newer absorptive style was more popular in America and Australia because it seemed to invite the participation and cooperation of the audience in a more egalitarian way. The actors acted like members of the same class or classes as the audience rather than imposing themselves as pseudo aristocrats. The stories that follow attempt to trace both successes and failures in this endeavor and to explain the reasons why.

CHAPTER 2

Pioneers

Mr. and Mrs. Stark

STANDING AT THE PROMPTER'S TABLE of Sydney's Royal Victoria Theatre on the evening of 14 June 1853, James Stark would have been thinking about the audience he could hear gathering. While he would have had a rehearsal that morning when actors' voices echoed off the empty benches, the theatre was now full of people, moving and talking. Stark's first task would be to find the right volume and pitch for his voice to carry clearly to them. Once he had done that, he could attend to his second and more important task: adjusting his performance to their responses so that they would accept him as a starring actor.

These would be the normal concerns for any leading actor appearing for the first time in any theatre in any location, but there were nuances in this situation that were abnormal. James Stark and his wife, Sarah Kirby, were the first stars from the American theatre to appear in Australia. Consequently, not only were they the first American actors to try to meet the theatrical and social expectations of Anglo-Australians, they were also the focus of whatever preconceived ideas and opinions members of the audience might have about the United States and its citizens.[1]

As established stars in San Francisco and Sacramento, the Starks had a reputation that would have preceded them because of the large number of miners migrating from the California to the Australian gold rush, and they had their own troubles with Australians. Sarah Kirby began acting in California at Rowe and Atwater's Olympic Amphitheatre in San Francisco, where her leading man was Francis Nesbitt McCron who, as Francis Nesbitt, had been the most popular leading actor in the colonies since 1842.[2] His alcoholic instability gradually cost him popularity, and in 1848, he headed for California. On 1 March 1850 as Richard III:

> Mr. McCron...presented himself before the audience in an improper condition. A difficulty occurred between him and Mrs. Kirby, an appeal to the audience was had and the dreadful question of nationality raised. Of course the audience sided with the lady. Mr. McCron was hissed, sought in vain to stem the disapprobation and was removed from the stage by the management.
>
> (*Alta*, 4 March)

Harmony must have been restored because these same actors played a season together at Sacramento's Tehema Theatre from 25 March until early June.[3] It was there that Sarah Kirby met James Stark. He had begun acting in 1846 and had learned his craft supporting some of the leading actors of the day: Edwin Forrest, Charles Kean, and J. W. Wallack.[4] He had been engaged by Charles R. Thorne as leading man for the Pacific Theatre in Sacramento, and when the season closed he was hired by Sarah Kirby, who was managing the competing Tehema Theatre.[5] An effective team, they went on to San Francisco, where Sarah Kirby's husband died in a street accident (*Alta*, 18 November 1850). Stark and Sarah Kirby were triumphantly received when they played on 16 January (*Alta*, 17 January 1851). They later married in Sacramento on 14 June 1851.[6]

In the meantime, she had been embroiled in a dispute with other Australians. On 14 January 1851, the actress Mrs. Hambleton poisoned herself. The cause, according to the *Alta California*, was the poor state of her marriage and her affection for Henry Coad, another actor in the company (15 January 1851), and her husband publicly accused Mrs. Kirby of having been the "fascinating serpent" responsible for turning his wife against him and arranging the liaison with Coad (*Picayune*, 15 January).

There is some evidence that their California troubles were known in Sydney. According to J. M. Forde ("Old Chum"), Thomas Willis, who had been an actor at the Olympic and was now in the company of the Royal Victoria, attempted to organize opposition (*Sydney Sportsman*, 2 October 1909). However, the only trouble reported in the Sydney papers of the day was between the management and some of the musicians. The Starks were received fairly and enthusiastically. Their popularity in Australia was equivalent to their popularity in California, and their reception established the first of the patterns that was to become typical for American players in Australia.

The *Herald* thought Stark "an actor of ordinary pretensions" and noted that his voice failed because of a cold. Even so, the *Herald* considered "his success may be pronounced to have been complete" (16 June 1853). This was the first of two visits to Australia together (1853–1854 and 1856–1857), and their reception, like the troubles that preceded their arrival, set a tone for those who followed.[7] They were the first actors with significant reputations in another country to visit Australia, and it was generally acknowledged that they were better than any who had been seen there before. As the American merchant George Francis Train reported from Melbourne:

> Mr. and Mrs. Stark are creating quite an excitement here. ...Our good people, in spite of their prejudices against Americans, acknowledge they never saw acting before. ...They have raised the tone of acting to a high standard at the Queen's Theatre.
>
> (*Alta*, 25 October 1853)

The plays the Starks offered in Australia were mostly the same ones they had performed in San Francisco, but the emphasis was different. Stark was best known for the title roles in Richelieu, Hamlet, and Ingomar the Barbarian. However, he also played Othello, Iago, Macbeth, Shylock, Lear, Richard III, and Petruchio. Mrs. Stark normally played Julie de Mortimer, Gertrude, Parthenia, Emelia, Lady Macbeth, Portia, Cordelia, and Lady Ann in the same plays.

In Australia, they played Shakespeare much less often than in California, and their most popular offering was *The Lady of Lyons*, which they performed nine times during their first visit. That was a far greater frequency than in San Francisco, and as late as 1868, the *Mercury* thought Claude Melnotte, "a part to which Mr. Stark's style of acting is well suited, and he sustained it throughout with much talent, being loudly applauded" (12 September 1868).

The Lady of Lyons by Edward Bulwer-Lytton had been written for William Charles Macready in 1838 and was regularly performed for the rest of the century. Both members of its romantic couple have mistaken notions about their social stations. Pauline, daughter of a high-middle-class couple, is encouraged to aspire to an aristocratic marriage, while she rejects Claude because he is the heir to a thrifty peasant, despite his accomplishments as a self-educated natural gentleman. Their eventual romance supporting honesty, fidelity, and class compatibility, must have appealed greatly to currency lads and lasses who saw themselves living in such a society.

As an actor, Stark was what Claude Melnotte was as a character: one who had improved himself through careful study and discipline. Thus, in this role, his stage presence matched his dramatic persona with particular accuracy. He was a predictable actor in the style of William Charles Macready. James Smith (Australia's dominant critic throughout the century) did not approve:

Mr. Stark will enable those who never had an opportunity…to form a very accurate notion of how Mr. Macready looked, walked, writhed his fingers, and broke his sentences up into ejaculatory fragments instead of punctuating them.

(*Argus*, 19 June 1856)

Even so, Smith found him "an actor of ability, earnestness, and intelligence." This was the tone of all his Australian reviews. The Empire thought him "the best 'good' Hamlet…for some time. …The prince seems 'made'—not 'born'" (24 April 1856), with which the *Argus* agreed, "In the soliloquies…there was…too much consciousness that his reveries…were anything but solitary" (21 June 1856). As late as 1868, Dr. James Neild, Melbourne's assistant coroner and Australia's most influential critic after James Smith, judged his Richelieu "a good, even, sustained piece of acting…so coherent and compact that it serves as a very good example of what may be done by well-applied industry" (*Australasian*, 13 June). Mrs. Stark was usually described as "chaste" and "appropriate," which meant that she did not offend. Although she was best liked in comic roles, the *Empire* thought, "The Gertrude of Mrs. Stark was well read, and most impressively acted throughout" (24 April 1856).

The only great defect was in their voices. Everyone noted it:

They have the peculiar Yankee nasal twang, to which it requires some time for an English ear to become reconciled. …They possess also a curious mode of pronunciation. …The word 'outrageous,' for instance, is pronounced 'outradjoos'—'fortune' becomes 'forchoon'. …Mr. Stark seems to be quite incapable of identifying himself with his subject; he merely acts acting. …Mr. Stark has the curious fashion, when excited, of wheezing very loudly at the end of each clause.

(Illustrated Sydney News, 8 April 1854)

The regular appearance of good British actors was probably behind the changes the Starks made in their repertory. For their first visit, they had anticipated their audience. They emphasized the non-Shakespearean part of the repertory, and observations about obtrusive accents occur seldom in reviews of those performances. During their second visit, they expanded that part of their repertory with such popular historical plays as *Pizarro*, *The Wife*, and *Lucretia Borgia*. Most importantly, they presented *Camille* for the first time in Australia.

In an age when leading roles were mostly male, a play featuring a female protagonist was novel. In this case, the sensation of the subject matter, the non-British origin, and the absence of previous performance all made Mrs. Stark's success more likely. Marguerite was the first role in which she had been singled out for unusual praise in San Francisco. The Australian papers disapproved of the play. Smith disliked it intensely, "How such a farrago of nonsense…could have met 'with distinguished success in Europe and the United States' we are at a loss to imagine" (*Argus*, 24 June 1856), and the audience seemed to agree. It played only twice in Melbourne. By contrast, it had played four nights in a row in San Francisco and six in Sydney. The writer for the *Herald* disliked the adaptation because it softened the "strong dark shade of guilt" of the French original. However, noting that the acting had to be good or that the audience would be "ennuied" by its four hours, he praised the climax:

> Earnestness and pathos are undoubtedly Mrs. Stark's best histrionic qualifications, and throughout the whole of the last act, lengthened as its dying scene was, to a degree

never perhaps witnessed in any former scenic representation, she commanded the silence of the house, and mastered the prolonged and dangerous situation in which the dramatist had placed her.

(10 May 1856)

The play's great popularity would come at the end of the decade because of the acting of Mary Provost.

James Stark made a further adjustment when he returned to Australia for his third visit, but while he offered fourteen plays from the traditional repertory, his featured vehicle was the contemporary American sensation melodrama, *Under the Gaslight* by Augustin Daly. Consequently, this final visit is better discussed in Chapter 5. Given the British domination of the Australian stage, Stark acted in an acceptable style, and modified his repertory to gain as much acceptance as possible during his first two visits. As a consequence, he experienced about the same degree of success in Australia as in California.

After their first visit to Australia, the Starks were reported to have claimed a clear profit of $10,000. It is unlikely that they made as much, or that they even made the claim. However, it was reported and believed. Thus, between the Stark's first two visits to Australia, more actors who played the same repertory arrived from America. McKean Buchanan came last and played the most performances. In between came briefer visits by Mr. and Mrs. Daniel Waller, Charles R. Thorne and his family, and the mismatched pair of Laura Keene and Edwin Booth. Though their receptions varied, none succeeded in the way the Starks had.

Their varying receptions suggest that in a community so isolated by distance from outside influence as Australia was, a key to popularity was novelty. The Wallers, Laura Keene, and Edwin Booth, however talented, were traditionally British in their repertory and style, whereas at least Kate Denin and McKean Buchanan offered the Australian audience something different.

The Wallers

Daniel Waller was an American who had played leading roles in the English provinces, and, in 1849, he married Emma Eardley of Sadler's Wells. They came to the United States in 1851 and toured as partners in the same repertory of tragedy and polite comedy as the Starks. They visited Australia between 12 June 1854 and November 1855, playing three engagements in Sydney, two each in Hobart and Melbourne. While they appeared in *Hamlet*, *Romeo and Juliet*, *Othello*, *The Hunchback*, and *Ingomar*, they were most popular in Lytton's comedy of *Money* (twenty-one performances) and Knowles's romance *Love* (fifteen). Neither was ever referred to as an "American," and there were no complaints about diction or phrasing. Their acceptance as British was confirmed in their final Melbourne engagement when Mrs. Waller appeared with the reigning British star of the Australian stage, Gustavus Vaughn Brooke.

The Thornes and Kate Denin

While the Wallers were away, Sydney theatres were dominated by Americans. Charles R. Thorne headed a company at the Royal Victoria. Their Australian visit was a single Sydney season (16 September to 11 December 1854), broken by the shift to another theatre on 23 October. At the end of that engagement, they moved to Malcolm's Amphitheatre (a circus arena) which they renamed the Royal Lyceum. They were succeeded at the Victoria by Laura Keene and Edwin Booth.

Thorne was a native of New York City. Before coming to California in 1850, he had acted and managed primarily at New York's Bowery and Chatham Gardens theatres, specializing in such equestrian melodramas as *El Hayder* and *Mazeppa*. Mrs. Thorne was a competent leading actress in mature roles, while daughter Emily was developing as an ingenue.

Kate Denin was the featured performer. Not only did she play Desdemona in *Othello*, Lady Anne in *Richard III*, and Julia in *The Hunchback*, but she regularly played men's roles: Rolla in *Pizzaro*, Claude Melnotte in *The Lady of Lyons*, Ruy Gomez in *Faint Heart Never Won Fair Lady*, as well as Prince Leander in the burlesque *The Invisible Prince*. This was a versatility, a range of persona that was unusual in any performer and something Australian audiences had not seen before. However, Thorne and Denin's greatest success was H. J. Conway's adaptation of *Uncle Tom's Cabin*, which will be treated with other productions of that play in Chapter 5.[8] Thus, novelty seems to have played a large part in their popularity.

Laura Keene and Edwin Booth

The brief appearances and indifferent receptions in Sydney and Melbourne of Laura Keene and Edwin Booth have puzzled their biographers, because she had learned her craft with Madame Vestris at London's Olympic Theatre, and he was the son of the legendary Junius Brutus Booth, rival of Edmund Kean on the London stage a generation earlier.

They played seven nights in Sydney (at the Royal Victoria, which competed with the Thornes at the Royal Lyceum) and five at the Queen's Theatre in Melbourne between 24 October and 24 November 1854 and repeated only two pieces (*Lady of Lyons* in Sydney and *Much Ado About Nothing* in Melbourne). Sydneysiders had the opportunity to see them in *Hamlet*, *The Merchant of Venice*, and *The Stranger*, opportunities denied the Melbourne audience.

Reviewing *Lady of Lyons*, Smith observed that "Although unheralded... Miss Keene and...Mr. Booth have achieved a most unequivocal success. ...The last scene of the play was a perfect triumph to Miss Keene" (*Argus*, 23 November 1854), and he thought that, "Mr. Booth's Benedick, some few national peculiarities of intonation apart, was very successful" (*Argus*, 21 November 1854). By contrast, the *Illustrated Sydney News* (which devoted the most attention to their visit) thought all was well. Her Beatrice was "delicately rendered, so finely delineated, so archly brought out," while his Benedick was "courtly, cavalier, love-proof, jaunty, humorous" (4 November 1854).

Although they had acted together, they were not well matched. She was scrupulous of her reputation and mature in her craft, while Booth was still raw, careless in his behavior on and off stage, a decade away from becoming America's leading tragedian, and in both cases they played in a repertory and style that would have been all too familiar to Australians. Moreover, as the *Argus* noted, Australian theatres were full of recently arrived British and American actors (4 November 1854). It was doubtless the combination of personal antipathy and professional difficulty that sent them back to America so quickly. The wonder was why they ever teamed up in the first place.[9]

McKean Buchanan

As these early instances indicate, actors from the States fell into two categories. They were either identifiable as "Yankees" or they were acceptable as Britons, depending on their repertory, their style of playing, or their accents. No one was more of a Yankee than the irrepressible

McKean Buchanan. A colorful individual who came to the stage as a passionate amateur from a mercantile background, he did no apprenticeship, he studied with no one. After success in amateur theatricals in New Orleans, he took to the professional stage. By the time he arrived in Australia he had acted all over the United States and Great Britain with considerable success.[10]

Buchanan stayed the longest (103 nights of playing), offered the largest repertory (24 main pieces), and the highest percentage of Shakespearean performance (45 percent). He played Hamlet most often (eleven times). Among the other standards he played Richelieu and Pizarro most often. In genteel comedy he emphasized Sir Harcourt Courtley in *London Assurance*.

Although his second visit (23 June 1860 to 26 March 1861) was shorter (80 nights), his repertory was as large, though changed to introduce his daughter, Virginia. Performances of plays by Shakespeare were nearly half the total (39 nights), but the most favored ones were new: *Julius Caesar* and *Comedy of Errors* featuring Virginia as Portia and Adriana. In both visits, Buchanan appeared with Gustavus Vaughn Brooke. They had alternated Othello and Iago during the first visit (21 and 22 April 1857), and Brooke again played Iago to Buchanan's *Othello* on 18 October 1860.

Dr. Neild's description of Othello, as well as providing physiological detail, is practically a catalogue of every objection ever recorded to Buchanan's acting, but it also makes it clear that his acting, however eccentric, was something different:

> Mr. Buchanan's Othello…is a very coarse and savage "man of color" who falls to swearing and profanity on the smallest provocation; who stamps his feet, grinds his teeth, and tears his hair on occasions of inconsiderable excitement; who is the unfortunate victim of epileptic convulsions which arrest the function of deglutition and

cause the secretion of the salivary glands to interfere materially with free and clear articulation; who gives ready ear to any tale impugning his wife's fidelity; who plans the murder of his lieutenant with a brutal ferocity, and who smothers the beautiful Desdemona as if he liked the operation.

(*My Notebook*, 25 April 1857)

For all the critical objection, Buchanan was popular. The number of performances attest to that, as do some notices that compare him favorably to his peers, such as this one of his Lear from the Mercury:

> Mr. Buchanan's representation of the sublime old British king is the finest and completest histrionic effort that has been presented on the modern stage. In comparison with it Mr. Brooke's impersonation seems, on remembrance, stagely and artificial enough, while Mr. Stark's performance comes to us as a mere idle impertinence.

(2 April 1857)

Genius or fraud, Buchanan was never dull. Like the Duke of Bilgewater and perhaps some other Americans, he "just knocked the spots out of any acting ever I seen before."[11]

CHAPTER 3

The Rise of the Emotional Actress, 1853–1860

Mary Provost and Avonia Jones

DISGUSTED BY BUCHANAN'S EXCESSES and disappointed in the abilities of American actors in general, Dr. Neild expected little from Mary Provost. Yet he soon proclaimed her a "genius."[1] She was the first of several young actresses to visit Australia whose repertory consisted primarily of suffering heroines and a few polite comedy ladies. It was a sub-set of the elite repertory adapted to the persona of the actress. The best-known Americans in this line of acting were Matilda Heron and Jean Davenport, but they did not travel down under. Mary Provost was both more successful and more versatile than her contemporaries, Annette Ince and Avonia Jones, who did. Moreover, she was the first American performer to play in Australia for several consecutive seasons, and her Australian residency was the high point of her career, patterns that repeat for others during the century.

A native of New York City, her first stage appearance at age fifteen was as Mariana in *The Wife* by Sheridan Knowles at the Chatham Theatre on 21 March 1848.[2] By the time she arrived in California she was married to the comedian J. P "Yankee" Addams and had become a star in the American South. She played in California as Mary Provost from 13 October 1856 to 31 July 1857, presumably shedding the husband along with his name. During her first engagement in Sacramento (November 1856) she met Samuel Colville, publisher of city directories and sometime actor, who became her manager and companion. Her repertory was unusually large (thirty-one roles). It was almost exactly divided between suffering heroines, such as Camille and comic ones, such as Peg Woffington in *Masks and Faces*.

She was praised for her originality and energy. Of her first appearance, as Parthenia, the *Alta* noted that she "introduced many new points, which we have never noticed as being given by any actress before. Her style and 'business' are entirely original" (14 October 1856). The next evening she appeared as Constance in *The Love Chase*, and the *Alta* noted that:

> It was a lively, vivacious and sprightly performance, and exhibited the versatility of the talent of Miss Provost in the performance of a character so opposite in many respects to that of Parthenia.

> (15 October 1856)

Although she played tragedy half the time, the *Alta* critic thought "her peculiar forte, as an actress, is exhibited in the light, attractive pieces" (9 November 1856), and praised her attempts in Shakespearean roles. As Juliet "her youthful, girlish appearance aided her much" (6 November 1856). Her Beatrice was a "graceful, vivacious piece of acting" (3 January 1857), while her Rosalind was "lively and agreeable in that lady's best style" (11 January 1857).

She and Colville spent a little more than three years in Australia, playing long seasons in Melbourne, Sydney, and the towns of Victoria. Her repertory was larger than in California (forty-three roles), but it exhibited the same variety. Although evenly divided between tragic and comic, the former were performed slightly more often. *Camille* and *Medea* were most frequent, followed by *Love. Andy Blake* and *Court and Stage* were her only comparable roles in comedy, but she often appeared in such farces as *Morning Call*, and *The Youth Who Never Saw Woman*.

Although Mrs. Stark first played it, Provost became identified with the role of Camille. Part of that identification arose from carefully managed publicity about her health. W. H. Ford, who acted with her, said that "she suffered much from consumption" ("Mummer Memoirs," *Sydney Sportsman*, 4 March 1908). Her playing of the role was universally praised as the best Australian audiences had seen, and long after she had departed, both James Smith and Dr. Neild continued to find other players of the role wanting by comparison.

Camille is a courtesan, who is transformed into an honest woman by the true love she shares with Armand Duval. However, once she understands that their liaison imperils both Armand's future and that of his sister, she sends him away and resumes her profession. Armand and Camille are reunited at her death bed, and while a happy ending is not possible (Camille's class can never be compatible with Armand's), forgiveness is, because Camille's sacrifice supported both marriage and class solidarity.

While some were offended by the subject matter, most regarded the play as highly moral. Camille was everything the middle class feared in a woman. She was the temptress, the false companion. Although she appeared attractive, she was destructive because her values were material and selfish. She became an object of sympathy when she renounced her former life. What made her a symbol of virtue was not her sexual fidelity to Armand, but her rejection of pleasure for domesticity, wealth for poverty, and the city for the country. Her ultimate sacrifice is to repel her beloved so that he will return to his family. Her conversion to bourgeois values is completed by her death: she is no longer an impediment to domestic virtue. Indeed, her stage life and death validate the values and institutions real courtesans threatened.

Provost first played the role in Australia at Bendigo where the paper reported "a pin might have been heard to drop...the sobs of several persons were distinctly audible" (*Bendigo Advertiser*, 27 August 1858). It was her death scene that both fascinated and repelled the critics. Dr. Neild provides a clinical description of it:

> I did not expect it,—and I did not want to see it. It is not art—it is artifice,—and in very bad taste. Here you may see, forsooth, life departing from the face—eyes glazing—final falling of the jaw. Thanks—but I'd rather not.
>
> (*My Notebook*, 10 July 1858)

In Melbourne, *The Age*'s critic found it "altogether too lugubrious and terrible...to please our peculiar taste" (25 March 1858).

In Sydney, Camille became the focus of a campaign against her. Mr. and Mrs. Charles Poole were lessees of the Prince of Wales Theatre in March 1859 when Colville took a lease on the neighboring Royal Victoria. In an apparent effort to frustrate the competing management, Mrs. Poole played Camille for the week before Provost's debut. This initiated a war of advertisements between the two managers, but once Provost had played the role, Mrs. Poole did not repeat it:

> There is reckless, sparkling gaiety about the Camille of this great American actress, which melts away, *malgre lui*, the cold reserve of the sternest moralist; a joyous abandon and willful prettiness in all she says and does. ...Miss Provost always fills up what has hitherto been a mere outline, leaving it instinct with grace, and life, and fiery energy.
>
> (*SMH*, 15 March 1859)

By contrast, Sydney's other daily paper, *The Empire*, sniffed, "We object to the work…as portraying scenes that excite rather our disgust than our sympathy. …The…admiration accorded to 'Camille,' is owing solely to the almost awe-inspiring personation of Miss Provost" (30 May 1859).

It requires only a little imagination to extract from these responses a sense of Mary Provost's acting in her most popular role. She was highly versatile. Her success in comedy and burlesque suggests an ability to switch moods quickly from comic abandon to real suffering. She seems to have infused fierce energy into carefully and elaborately detailed physical characterizations. The combination of energy and detail seemed to achieve a precarious balance, absorptive for most, but objectionably reflective for some. She seems to have been an exciting, exotic visitor to the parlor.

In a letter to James Smith, Provost objected not to Mrs. Poole's competing with her, but to the theft of her intellectual property:

> Mr. Poole of the "Prince of Wales" had *Camille* put in immediate rehearsal, and produced it with Mrs. Poole as Camille, purposely to destroy, if possible, the effect of my opening night. That, I thought nothing of, it was a matter of business.—When Mr. Downey, who is the Prompter at the Prince of Wales (and who also prompted at the "Princess" in Melbourne, during my engagement,) betrayed to Mrs. Poole, not only my stage business, but even the modified language which I introduced into the play myself, as well as the minute details of action, etc., I was grieved to the heart, notwithstanding my contempt for the woman, who is so little of an artist, as to pilfer in a few hours, what it has cost me days, weeks, months, years to comparatively perfect.
>
> (4 March 1859)[3]

To their regret, this was not the end of Colville and Provost's dealings with the Pooles.

After three months in Sydney she returned to Victoria, and then began a second Sydney season at the Royal Victoria on 10 October 1859, where they became embroiled in Poole's managerial difficulties. Poole owed salaries to members of the company that Colville refused to pay. He offered them work instead, and some accepted but others didn't. This led to a disturbance on 26 November when Provost and the ex-strikers played *Camille*. The disaffected actors occupied the pit and shouted the performance down (*SMH*, 28 November 1859). Poole claimed to be too ill to attend to matters of business, but eventually declared bankruptcy. By Boxing Day, Colville controlled both theatres, and Provost appeared at both. Appearing in holiday season farces, she opened at the Prince of Wales in *The Maid of Munster* and closed at the Victoria with *Perfection* and *Nature and Philosophy*.

Settled in Sydney, her Medea and her Phaedra were well-received, but her two greatest successes were by Dion Boucicault. She excelled in his pathetic *Janet Pride*, which had recently run for a hundred nights at London's Adelphi Theatre, and in which she appeared in a dual role as mother and daughter. She also sparkled in his Irish farce, *Andy Blake*. After her death, Dr. Neild remembered that she was "the only actress who ever played Andy Blake to my satisfaction" (*Australasian*, 18 December 1875). Her season finally ended early in September of 1860.

She departed for a brief engagement in Melbourne, almost certainly to avoid direct competition and comparison with Avonia Jones. While Provost was not averse to rivalry when she was the newcomer, she was probably loath to risk it when she was the shining star. Rivalry was, as Provost had observed to Smith, a matter of business, and she could not have been surprised that two of her contemporaries had followed her to Australia.

Annette Ince, daughter of Baltimore theatre manager George Ince, specialized in the tragic part of the emotional repertory, appearing most often as Julia in *The Hunchback*. The reviewer for the *Alta* approved of her acting, frequently terming it "correct," "chaste," and "elegant." There was never any mention of energy or strong feeling. Although successful in California, she failed drastically during a two-week engagement at Melbourne's Theatre Royal and returned almost at once to California where she continued to play until the end of the Civil War.

James Smith's review of her opening performance as Julia clearly blames her failure on her reflective "American" style of playing:

> Miss Ince's style of acting belongs to that of a highly arti-
> ficial school, of which numerous disciples have visited
> this colony from the United States. …Every tone and
> gesture is studiously appropriate, and the strength and
> duration of every emotion exactly calculated before it is
> displayed, but there is an utter absence of spontaneity, of
> natural impulse, and unaffected feeling.
>
> (*Argus*, 3 May 1858)

Avonia Jones was a more serious rival. Her mother, Melinda, was a formidable player of heavy male and female roles, while her father, George, was later notorious as the eccentric "Count Johannes," whose career resembled that of Mark Twain's Duke of Bilgewater. Her mother was responsible for training Avonia and acted as her manager. At least one colleague, Walter Leman, thought she would have been better without the coaching, "Mrs. Melinda taught her to over-act, which propensity is not uncommon among the members of the profession, and was always a marked peculiarity of Mrs. Jones."[4]

Like Annette Ince, she stayed on the emotional side of the repertory, performing Medea, Camille, Lucretia Borgia, and Juliet most frequently. In the last, she sometimes played opposite Melinda as Romeo. Like Provost and Ince, she had starred all through the Ohio Valley and the southern states and had a successful season in California before beginning her Australian campaign in Melbourne. The reviewer for the *Alta* thought that as Juliet, "She was exceedingly effective, particularly in the representation of passionate love" (14 May 1859). He also praised her Lady Teazle. She "manifested her great abilities in the calmer and more subdued walks of genteel comedy, and her manifestations of womanish pique lent a great charm to her endeavor" (15 July 1859).

Her reception in Melbourne was more enthusiastic than Mary Provost's had been. James Smith compared her Medea to that of Rachel and Ristori (*Argus*, 28 February 1860), and his description of her Camille made it clear that it was similar to Provost's, "The cough, the distressing symptoms of disease and death were too painfully obtrusive" (*Argus*, 15 March 1860). The reviewer for the Sydney Empire offered a direct comparison of the two Medeas that was in Jones's favor, "Miss Provost's is more laboured— more finished by art—and in many portions, more artificial. Miss Jones disdains stage trickery, and in her evident hatred of it, often refuses to make a point" (11 September 1860), while the *Sydney Mail* was reminded of the great American actress Charlotte Cushman by Jones's playing of Bianca in *The Italian Wife*. Both Smith and the critic for the *Empire* agreed that Margaret Elmore in *Love's Sacrifice* was not only her best role, but that her interpretation was the best Australia had seen—better, by implication, than Provost's.

She attracted the attention of Gustavus Vaughn Brooke, the dominant actor of the period in Australia. She toured with him, was a feature of his final seasons in Melbourne, left for England with him, and married him there.

No account of the Australian careers of Avonia Jones and Mary Provost is complete without an understanding of the constant tension that prevailed in the relationship between them. Some tension would have been natural. They were about the same age, and they played similar repertories for the same audiences. But that, as Provost had observed about Mrs. Poole's playing of Camille, was simply a matter of "business." It was to be expected.

However, there were personal and professional issues that exacerbated this tension between them. As a matter of business, they did not compete directly. When Avonia Jones came to Sydney, Mary Provost went to Melbourne. Moreover, each expressed a grudging admiration of the other in letters to James Smith. When Jones first appeared, Provost wrote:

> I am glad Miss Jones has been successful as she is a coun-
> trywoman, and because she evidently deserves it. But I
> never heard of her as an actress except by word from
> California, which said that although she was worthy of it,
> she did not receive her meed [sic] of encouragement from
> the public.
>
> (17 November 1859)[5]

In a similar vein, Jones wrote Smith:

> I saw Miss Provost play "Rosalind," last Monday, and
> four characters were doubled in the play. With Miss
> Provost I was very much pleased, and was very sorry that
> after this night she withdrew, as I anticipated much
> pleasure during the week.
>
> (6 September 1860)

However, these professionally polite attitudes masked deeper feelings. As managers, Colville and Provost had wanted to engage Jones to play at their Sydney theatre, the Victoria. Negotiations were troublesome:

> I think the young lady as you say is badly advised. If she had a more judicious parent, it would have been better for her. But I have made her an offer, and want her to play Camille—advised her by all means to come to Sydney (through her agent, of course) but she wants extensive terms which, as she cannot, or at least has failed to draw in California and Melbourne—it would not do to give. She wrote that she had done a great business in Melbourne but that was another very silly mistake—as we had already learned that she injured the "Treasury" materially.
>
> (31 March 1860)

Jones finally did come to an arrangement with Colville through the efforts of the actor W. H. Stephens who sublet the theatre, but the actress continued to accuse both Colville and Provost of dishonest dealings with her (31 August 1860).

Perhaps at the bottom of this sea of ill-feeling was Provost's frustrated desire to play opposite Brooke—something Jones had achieved without apparent effort. Colville had asked Smith to negotiate on their behalf (21 May 1859), but nothing came of it, although Provost wrote of her "strong desire" to play with Brooke (26 August 1859). The tragedian was unresponsive, and Provost became convinced that the Pooles and others had spoken ill of her to Brooke (17 January 1860).

Adding insult to injury, while Jones's romance with Brooke flourished, Provost seemed domestically embarrassed. Yankee Addams (her former husband) arrived in Sydney after a brief, inconclusive engagement in Melbourne. Although he did not act, his presence seems to have affected Provost. As Jones reported to Smith:

Colville is very unpopular and so is Miss Provost, for they are tired of her. Since Mr. Addams arrived, she has thrown off all disguise, and passes as Mrs. Colville, wears a wedding ring, and lives with him as his wife.

(10 August 1860)

In the end Jones and Brooke sailed away, while Provost and Colville remained together. He was still her manager when she was reported to have married G. W. Brown, Jr. in Davenport, Iowa (*New York Clipper*, 23 January 1864).

Both actresses continued their careers in the United States. Jones's repertory remained largely unchanged, and she had a successful engagement at Wallack's Theatre, New York City, in the summer of 1864. Although she continued playing in the English provinces after Brooke drowned on a return voyage to Australia, she seemed dispirited and soon died.

After a brief London engagement in January 1862, Provost returned to the American provinces where she was especially successful as Bob Brierly in *The Ticket of Leave Man*. On 15 September 1865, she signed a contract with George Coppin, acting as agent for William Hoskins, manager of the Haymarket Theatre, Melbourne, to play four weeks beginning 29 January 1866, "in New Dramas and Yankee Gal Farces to be provided by Miss Provost."[6] She did not keep the engagement, although it was reported that she went to England in 1868 to further the career of her daughter, Violet Colville.

CHAPTER 4

Child Prodigies

Anna Maria Quinn

ALTHOUGH NO MORE THAN FOURTEEN when she first acted, Mary Provost was not the youngest performer, American or otherwise, to appear in Australia. Whether it was in the London blacking factory, or the mills of Lowell, children regularly worked for wages in the Victorian era, and audiences seemed to have an endless appetite for what Dickens caricatured in the person of Miss Ninetta Crummles, "the infant phenomenon," deprived of sleep and fed "an unlimited allowance of gin-and-water from infancy."[1] Perhaps the most successful child actors were Ruth and Ellen Bateman, but they never visited Australia. The subjects of this chapter did, and one achieved notable success as an adult performer and manager.

Anna Maria Quinn was a typical child prodigy. Most likely she was born in St. Louis in 1848 and first went on the stage there at the theatre where her mother was the costumer (*Illustrated Sydney News*, 23 December 1854). She appeared in San Francisco in 1854 under the tutelage of the actor James Vinson, "one of the best delineators of old men on the stage" (*Alta*, 8 July 1854), who was regularly referred to as her guardian. She became a featured attraction, playing Hamlet in the first act from that play at both the Metropolitan and Union theatres, and it was as Hamlet that Vinson presented her at Sydney's Royal Lyceum, 27 December 1854. She played there, in Hobart, Melbourne, and regional Victoria until the end of February 1857. She then proceeded to London and New York, returning to Melbourne in May of 1858. This seems to have been the end of her juvenile career, and a year later it was reported that her father had been appointed "clerk of the Bench of Magistrates at Beechworth" (*SMH*, 4 April 1859).

Although Hamlet drew the most attention, she also played Portia in the trial scene from *The Merchant of Venice*, Young Norval in the first act of *Douglas*, and Lady Gay Spanker in the third act of *London Assurance*. However, the roles she played most frequently were in farce afterpieces: Maria in *The Actress of All Work* by W. H. Oxberry, in which she played six different characters. Of her performance in that play, *The Era* wrote:

> In each of the six personations she has to assume, Miss Quinn displayed considerable spirit and ability, and dashed off the whole set of characters with a great deal of life and piquancy, while in two of the assumptions, Flourish and Lounge, she exhibited talent of a much higher order. ...She has a good figure, pleasing and well marked features, with very expressive eyes; she treads the stage with confidence and grace, and her action is natural and easy.[2]

Other farces in which she was featured included *To Parents and Guardians*, *The Spoiled Child*, *A Middy Ashore*, and *Nan, the Good for Nothing*. She also appeared as Little Eva in *Flowers from Uncle Tom's Cabin*, an adaptation of scenes from the novel created for her by Frank Fowler.[3]

Her reception was most favorable in the farces. She was regarded as the principal attraction on the bill of the newly opened Theatre Royal, Melbourne, in 1855. The critic for The Age reported that she was "applauded to the echo for her clever and versatile assumption of...half a dozen characters" (18 July), and the *Argus* noted with approval that:

> Her exhibition…is not characterised by the imposition of that rather painful impression which precocious talent is apt to confer. Her assumption of six characters with the quick changes…proved the great ability of this intelligent child.
>
> (19 July)

The Age, however, dismissed her Hamlet as, "Chiefly remarkable as an act of memory and as an exhibition of her knowledge of stage business. In other respects we cannot approve of so young a child undertaking a character so philosophical…and so arduous" (11 August), and later observed that, "To our English taste, Americanisms are exaggerated enough at all times…to us it appears a distortion of the grotesque" (11 May 1858).

On this note, her juvenile career seems to have closed, and she did not act for five years. Her return as an adult came in the role of Lady Gay Spanker in Boucicault's *London Assurance. The Age* was pleased with her person, "She has grown to be a tall and graceful woman, with no inconsiderable personal attractions, correct enunciation, and undoubted knowledge of stage effect," but it thought that her voice "hardly of sufficient strength to render, with due effect some passages" (8 May 1863).

From September of 1863 through February of the following year she was a member of the resident company at Sydney's Prince of Wales Theatre, supporting the American star Joseph Jefferson in *Rip Van Winkle*, *Our American Cousin*, and *The Ticket of Leave Man*, and Charles Kean in *Louis XI* and *King Lear*. She made a starring visit to Adelaide between March and June of 1866 where she attempted to establish herself in the modern emotional repertory, appearing as Lady Audley, Camille, and Pauline (*Lady of*

Lyons). However, the *Advertiser's* notices were merely polite.

She was then engaged by Mr. and Mrs. Charles Vincent (Louisa Cleveland) at Melbourne's Princesses Theatre where her most frequent appearances were in Byron's burlesques (Leonora in *Ill-Treated-Trovatore* and Rowena in *Ivanhoe*). Her one success there in the emotional repertory came as Barbara Hare, the ingenue in *East Lynne*, "A careful and discriminating piece of acting" (*Argus*, 10 September 1866). Her other notices were similar. Finally, the critic for *The Age* seemed to lose patience. Reviewing *Hamlet*, he complained, "Miss Quinn's Ophelia, careful and all too studied, was an impersonation into which one little touch of nature would have thrown some light. Why can't this young lady try to get off her stilts?" (4 March 1867). Afterwards, "She settled down as a respectable stock actress, in one of the many companies which made money—and heaps of it—in touring the mining towns of Victoria and New Zealand, chiefly in the latter where money was very plentiful in the sixties)."[4] She eventually returned to the United States where she continued to play with limited success.

Louise Arnott

Her contemporary, Louise Arnott, arrived in Australia as a member of George W. Marsh's Juvenile Comedians. Arnott's career resembled Quinn's. She starred as a juvenile in Sydney and Melbourne from 24 June 1861 until 31 March 1863. The Marsh troupe returned to San Francisco where it disbanded a year later. In this phase of her career, she played male roles opposite her sister, Jenny (William in *Black Eyed Susan*, Don Caesar in *Don Caesar de Bazan*, Claude Melnotte in *The Lady of Lyons*, Julian Dormilly in *Six Degrees of Crime*), but she also played principal female roles opposite either G. W. Marsh, the younger, or Louis Aldrich (Lady Macbeth, Lurline in *The Naiad Queen*). The company was favorably reviewed, though it is clear that, as in Quinn's case, admiration was based mostly on the phenomenon of juvenile players in adult roles.

She returned to Sydney in August of 1864 to attempt the transition to an adult actress. At first, she repeated her breeches roles, but then settled in as an ingenue, playing Ophelia and Desdemona. In May and June of 1865, she was in Brisbane where she was featured as Lady Audley and as May Edwards (*Ticket of Leave Man*). It was also here that she received her first enthusiastic notices. The *Courier* thought that "On the stage her personnel [sic] is all that can be desired; her intonation is clear and distinct and her acting graceful, natural, and unconstrained" (20 May), but the houses were small, "Some of the best works…have been played to a smaller average attendance than might be expected at a second or third rate provincial theatre in England after the close of the seasons" (*Courier*, 17 June). However, after a brief season in Sydney, she returned to Queensland for an extended season (9 December 1865 to 26 February 1866, followed by two months of touring in the countryside). Her repertory continued to feature male roles in burlesque, as well as ingenues in Irish pieces (Judy O'Trot in *Ireland As It Is*, Nellie O'Neill in *The Green Bushes*, Anne Chute in *The Colleen Bawn*).

Toward the end of her Australian career, she came to the fore at Melbourne's Princesses Theatre in burlesque (Burnand's *Wreck Ashore* and *Ixion*, Byron's *Princess Springtime and his Lady Belle Belle*, or *Fortunio*). It is in Dr. Neild's reviews that one finds the first clear descriptions of her acting: "Her vocal mannerisms are as unpleasing as ever; her pathos is accompanied by audible inspirations, and she employs that peculiar masculine intonation" (*Australasian*, 11 August 1866); "She is graceful, and has an expressive face. ...Her action is so natural as to be free from any...staginess. But when she speaks one cannot help being...irritated and disappointed. ...Miss Arnott exhibits inaccuracies of pronunciation due, of course, to her nationality" (*Australasian*, 31 August 1867). However, illustrating once again different standards in different communities, she was praised repeatedly during an engagement in Adelaide. *The Advertiser* found her "pleasant," "spirited," and "arch."

Her last Australian engagement was supporting Americans H. F. and Amy Stone in 1867, and she went with them to Shanghai. She later managed a variety theatre in Victoria, British Columbia, and continued acting in the United States for twenty years.

Josephine Gougenheim

The dominant juvenile from America with the longest, most notable Australian career was Josephine Gougenheim. Born in England, she made her first appearance on the stage with her older sister, Adelaide, in the farce *Perfection* at Burton's Theatre, New York City, 20 August 1850, at the age of seven. During the season of 1854, Joey had become a "mainstay" of the company at New York's Broadway Theatre in farces. After a benefit at the end of May, the sisters headed for California where they appeared triumphantly in August.

They were foils for each other. Adelaide was slightly shorter, with a fuller figure, a low-pitched mellow voice, and a natural manner. Joey was more energetic and was considered artificial in contrast to her sister. James Smith describes the contrast better than anyone:

Miss [Adelaide] Gougenheim has an expressive face, an elegant carriage, and considerable power in depicting the softer passions. Her bye-play is good, and her performances are always finished and well sustained. The style of Miss Joey is totally different: she is all dash, and throws off her words and action in the most vivacious, rattling, ad capiandum manner possible. Not a gesture or a tone, for all this, which does not seem to have been diligently rehearsed and studied. She has another peculiarity, not a good one we think, of all on a sudden discharging every atom of expression from her countenance, ignoring all idea of bye-play, and becoming a sort of stage statue for a second or two, until it is her turn to speak again. Her action, overwhelmingly vivacious and showy, is not sustained. You have first a flash of lightning, then a little feminine thunder, a clouded brow, and a ringing laugh, each excellently thrown in, and then, the next moment, a total lapse. The electricity is gone and there an end.

(*Argus*, 30 July 1857)

While Joey played in over one hundred-fifty pieces during her career, her two standards were period theatrical comedies by Tom Taylor. In *Court and Stage*, she played the Restoration actress Nell Gwynne, and while they were together, Adelaide played the role of Frances Stewart. The sisters were similarly joined in Taylor's *Masks and Faces*, in which Joey played the Georgian actress Peg Woffington, while Adelaide played Mabel Vane. The other roles that she played throughout were Don Leander in Planche's *The Invisible Prince*, Norah in Boucicault's *The Irish Heiress*, and Dot in *The Cricket on the Hearth*. In the 1860s, she had great success in the melodramas *The Woman in White* (Marion Halcomb) and *Life in the South* (Capitola Black).

They sailed for Australia on 7 August 1856 and opened at Sydney's Royal Lyceum on 6 October. Transferring to the Royal Victoria at the beginning of December, they played until 12 January 1857. In addition to the Tom Taylor comedies and the burlesques of *Invisible Prince* and *Cinderel-*

la, they appeared most often in Knowles's *The Love Chase* (Adelaide as Lydia, Joey as Constance). They were ignored by the *Herald* and praised in generic terms by *The Empire*. When they moved on to Hobart for a month, the *Mercury* was delighted. Of "Miss Ady," it thought "Her acting is exceedingly dignified—and her voice rich and musical," while of Joey, it wondered, "Who that heard her on Friday night, but has her loud and joyous laugh still ringing in their ears?" (9 February 1857).

Melbourne was altogether different, and on its face, the record is puzzling. After playing two and a half months in Sydney and a solid two weeks in Hobart, they appeared for three nights (25–27 May 1857) in *Court and Stage* at the Princesses Theatre and returned to Sydney where they played through June and then toured the Victorian gold fields. With apparent satisfaction, the *Age* reported that they played "to such meager audiences as must have satisfied both of these artistes that the Californian system of puffery does not go down here" (29 May), probably an allusion to the breathless, *Histrionic Memoir of the Misses Adelaide and Joey Gougenheim with Opinions of the Press* which their agent circulated in advance, while James Smith merely noted their "marked peculiarities of voice and manner" (*Argus*, 26 May). Acknowledging their personal charm, Dr. Neild was equally reserved:

> If a rapid letter-perfect delivery of the text, without feeling, humor, or genuine vivacity be the excellence of impersonation, then I acquiesce in the opinion of the play bills; if a stiff mechanical action be the supreme merit of histrionic display, then I have nothing to say.
>
> (*My Notebook*, 30 May 1857)

Given this response, their reappearance on 29 July at the same theatre under their own management seems surprising, but they triumphed.

Their repertory was an astute blend of polite comedy, farce, and burlesque. Apart from their popularity as performers, the sisters were repeatedly commended for the care with which they managed the scenery, costumes, and music. Summing up their season, Dr. Neild wrote:

> They have produced four or five sterling comedies, as many pieces of less pretensions, but excellent of their kind, and four extravaganzas; and they have done this within three months; and all these have been produced in a style that, I hesitate not to say, were the remarkable fact known in London, would bring them over the wide ocean that divides us as many bouquets of perennial flowers as the Princess's theatre could hold.
>
> (*My Notebook*, 24 October 1857)

In spite of their success, Joey held a grudge which she stated in her curtain speech at their closing performance prior to the Christmas season:

> It is a hard thing, Ladies and Gentlemen, for Stars to come so many thousand miles and be shut out of the great city of these colonies: to find that they must either accept an engagement which would scarcely defray their expenses in your city, or else be forced to pass it by altogether.
>
> (*Age*, 26 October 1857)

The object of Joey's remarks was the managerial team of George Coppin and Gustavus Vaughn Brooke. The latter responded in the papers two days later, claiming that the sisters had been made a fair offer, which they had rejected, and he published the relevant correspondence as proof of his claim. They had requested half the gross receipts per night, and Coppin had countered with an offer of either half the net receipts or £100 per night and two half benefits (*Age*, 28 October 1857). Joey retorted that they had only asked for the same terms that Coppin gave Brooke (*Age*, 29 October 1857).

The matter was more complex than a disagreement over terms. Desirous to play Melbourne, and displeased with Coppin's offer, they contracted with John Black, then managing Astley's Amphitheatre as The Princesses Theatre. When they arrived, they found that Black could not or would not meet the terms of the agreement, and he obtained a writ upon their possessions when they terminated their engagement. To gain their freedom, they paid Black a substantial sum and agreed not to appear in Melbourne for six months.[5] To what extent Coppin may have been party to Black's actions is unknown, but apparently Joey held him responsible for their troubles.

While no one could compete with Brooke in the classic male repertory, the Gougenheims offered audiences a clear alternative until 6 March 1858 when, after another tour of the goldfields, they returned to the United States. Reprising their Australian career and its difficulties, which included "the bitter spirit manifested on several occasions by the press," the *Age* concluded:

> It speaks well for the appreciation of talent in these colonies that the Misses Gougenheim have, within two years, played nearly 500 nights; and this, perhaps, is the strongest inducement that could be held out for other artists to visit our shores.

> (8 March 1858)

The Gougenheims continued together until Adelaide's marriage and retirement a year later. On her own, Joey's American career did not prosper. She played in the South during the early part of the Civil War, but that part of the nation quickly became unprofitable. She returned to San Francisco, but she terminated her engagement because she refused to play on Sundays (a normal performance day in

California at the time). She and her manager, R. A. Eddy, departed suddenly for Australia, owing, it was said, $1,600 in salaries to actors they had engaged (letter from Sheridan Corbyn, dated 21 January 1862 in *New York Clipper*, 29 February 1862).

She resumed her Australia career as Hester Grazebrook in Tom Taylor's *An Unequal Match*, on 13 March 1862 at Melbourne's Royal Princesses' Theatre. She played steadily throughout the colonies for the next two and a half years. In addition to *The Woman in White* and *The Unequal Match*, she added Boucicault's *Janet Pride* to fill out the emotional side of her repertory. She retained the Taylor comedies and *The Irish Heiress* from before and added *The Field of the Cloth of Gold* to her burlesque offerings.

She continued to be favorably received on the whole, but there was always criticism and critical controversy. For example, in Sydney, *The Empire* thought her Hester Grazebrook "Exquisitely…played, no claptrap effect, no glitter, nothing but…gentleness and womanly affection" (13 October 1862), but her performance of that role was judged too artificial in Melbourne:

> Miss Gougenheim's village beauty and rural gaucherie…resembled what it purported to represent only to the same extent that the shepherds and shepherdesses of Watteau and Boucher resembled French peasants.
>
> (*Argus*, 14 March 1862)

The same judgment was shared in Adelaide, and while *The Advertiser* praised the "power and success" of her Janet Pride (29 September 1863), it continued to prefer her Peg Woffington and Nell Gwynne (21 October 1863).

It was in this period that she appeared in classical roles opposite some of the best English actors to visit Australia. Her first such engagement was with Charles Warner in

Hobart. Here, she first appeared as Desdemona and Katherine, Luciana (*Comedy of Errors*), and a single performance as Lydia Languish. She then appeared with Barry Sullivan, the acknowledged successor to Brooke, at Melbourne's Theatre Royal, as Ophelia (11 August) and Desdemona (4 September 1862). In these and similar roles, she was usually described as adequate. She also supported the American star Joseph Jefferson during an engagement in Sydney.

After her marriage to Marmaduke Constable (8 July 1865), she performed only occasionally. Her last appearance in Melbourne was in the Christmas pantomime of *Sinbad*, and Dr. Nield reported that "she has lost much of the dash and fire that once characterised her. She is correct and staid...almost prim indeed, but primness and burlesque are incompatibles" (*Australasian*, 2 January 1869). She had month-long seasons in Sydney in 1869 and 1871, and her last appearance in Sydney was for three performances in mid-May of 1879 when she reprised her three most successful parts, Nora, Nell, and Peg.

Doubtless because her husband owned property in Queensland, she appeared for several seasons in Brisbane during the 1870s, but her most notable season during the 1870s was in the New South Wales gold rush town of Gulgong, where she was the moving force behind a theatre for the first half of 1872. It was presumably she and her company that Anthony Trollope referred to when he recorded a performance of *The Colleen Bawn* "acted with a great deal of spirit, and a considerable amount of histrionic talent."[6]

After the turmoil had ceased, she was remembered affectionately by "Autolycus" (James Smith) in his memoirs of "Melbourne in the Sixties":

Joey was a tall and exquisitely symmetrical beauty. Her large dark eyes shone...in a face of faultless outlines. ...Her voice was ineffably soft and mesmerically tender in tone. ...She was a charming lady in her nature and in her manner.

(Argus, 11 February 1905)

She was delightful in comedy.

As Norah Merrion in "The Irish Heiress," her native Dublin accent gave a special charm to the performance, always a favorite one with her audiences. "Nell" Gwynne was another part which she made distinctly interesting and popular.

(Argus, 8 October 1904).

However positive these memories might have been, Joey was buried alone in a grave in Sydney's Waverley Cemetery that is today unmarked.

CHAPTER 5

The American Idiom: Yankees and Slaves

FROM THE BEGINNING, American performers included in their repertory plays that represented America and Americans. Because the United States had a much larger, more diverse population spread over a greater area, its culture presented a series of novelties to Australia's more homogenous, more urbanized audience. However, there were elements in these representations of America that resonated with the colonial audience. These stories and their characters combined social value with novelty.

For the Anglo-Australian audience, the geography of the United States was divided into three regions: the North and West (New England and the Ohio River Valley), inhabited by the Yankee and the Frontiersman, respectively, and the South, inhabited by the African-American slave. Separately and together, these regions and their characters defined America for nineteenth-century Australians, especially in the performances of Joseph Jefferson and Hosea Easton, who benefited from their Australian residencies as much (or more) as any other American performers.

American characters first appeared on the English stage in Charles Mathews's three-and-a-half-hour solo performance, *Mathews in America* (1824), based on his tour as a performer the previous year.[1] Yankees, frontiersmen, African-Americans, and recent French and Irish immigrants were all ridiculed to shouts of laughter. American actors who specialized in Yankees and Frontiersmen soon followed: James H. Hackett (1833), George Handel Hill (1836), Danforth Marble (1844), Josh Silsbee (1851), Mr. and Mrs. William J. Florence and Mr. and Mrs. Barney Williams (1856). American representatives of African-Americans were a host of blackface performers, beginning with Thomas D. Rice (1836), and the Virginia Minstrels (1843).

The Yankee and the Frontiersman, both male and female, had much in common with each other and with other types familiar to Australians. They had evolved from the working-class characters of eighteenth-century farce afterpieces, whose manners and speech were cause for laughter, but whose honesty, loyalty, and bravery were cause for cheers. They were egalitarian in their manners, outlandish in their dress and speech. They exaggerated their own and their country's accomplishments. They drove a hard bargain and put their own interests first, but they had a natural sense of justice and were capable of courage and unselfish action on behalf of others. They were, in short, comic caricatures of the natural lady and gentleman of the Romantic imagination.[2]

The appeal of such potentially anarchic characters to audiences conditioned by a culture based on hereditary classes can be sensed in Taylor's *Our American Cousin* (1861), in which Asa Trenchard (a combination of Yankee and Frontiersman), sacrifices a fortune for the love of a proper English girl: "I'm a rough sort of a customer, and don't know much about the ways of great folks, I've got a cool head, a stout arm, and a willing heart, and I think I can help you, just as one cousin ought to help another" (*II. i*).

The appeal of the African-American character was similar. Current scholarship makes a strong case that blackface minstrelsy extended the tradition of working-class humor in early nineteenth-century British farce afterpieces. In this view, blackface makeup was a protective mask to hide the identity of the subversive trickster. It was not an expression of sympathy with the plight of black persons in either America or Great Britain. It united members of the working class both in an expression of disrespect for authority and in a feeling of innate superiority over persons of color.[3]

In the American drama, these regional types frequently appeared together. Both Anna Cora Mowatt's *Fashion* (*Olympic*, 1850) and Samuel Woodworth's *The Forest Rose* (*Adelphi*, 1851) contained Yankee and African-American characters. The most frequently performed American play, *Uncle Tom's Cabin*, also offered multiple characters of each type. Between September of 1852 and February of 1853, twelve versions of Mrs. Stowe's novel appeared on the London stage.[4] A similar blend of characters is found in Boucicault's *The Octoroon* (1861).

In addition to these appeals, *Uncle Tom's Cabin* confirmed the British sense of national superiority to the United States based on their earlier abolition of the slave trade. As N. W. Senior pointed out:

> The evil passions which *Uncle Tom's Cabin* gratified in England were not hatred or vengeance, but national jealousy and national vanity. We have long been smarting under the conceit of America—we are tired of hearing her boast that she is the freest and the most enlightened country that the world has ever seen. …All parties hailed Mrs. Stowe as a revolter from the enemy. …She taught us how to prove that democrats may be tyrants, that an aristocracy of caste is more oppressive than an aristocracy of station.[5]

Prior to 1880, Australia's America was a reflection of Great Britain's. Colonists shared the British attitude of moral superiority to Americans, and they brought British class distinctions and racial attitudes with them to the Antipodes. If anything, their prejudices were even stronger because the working class was made up almost entirely of descendants of convicts and the Irish. Moreover, Anglo-Australians had an indigenous population to deal with, and Australian history is as replete with stories of the destruction of an indigenous culture as that of the United States. White Australians' attitudes toward Aboriginal Australians, their fear of rebellion and miscegenation, resembled those of antebellum American whites.

Uncle Tom's Cabin and *The Octoroon* were more complex in their appeal to the nineteenth-century audience than they seem now. On the one hand, light-complexioned slaves (George, Eliza, and Zoe) look, speak, and act white. A European audience would approve of their aspirations for economic justice, family solidarity, and romance as they would of their own. On the other hand, the blackface slaves in *Uncle Tom's Cabin* and *The Octoroon* are content. Uncle Tom, for example, is a person of responsibility and authority under his first two masters. Both villains, Simon Legree and Jacob McClosky, are Northerners; they do not belong to or understand the system, and so they pervert it. Thus, suffering and death are not an indictment of the institution of slavery, but of an outsider who does not understand the working of the system.[6]

One can see that the plays appealed to several different sets of values at the same time. While these values may not have been consistent or coherent with one another, it seems likely that most members of the audience shared some or all of them. Australian and American cultures were enough alike that many of these appeals appear to have been at work in both places. The great pastoral stations of Australia were similar to antebellum Southern plantations. The station was a large area of land, operated for profit, and often employed Aboriginal Australians in conditions resembling slavery.

The system of assigning convicts to work for private persons, in effect after 1820, functioned as a form of slavery, and the classic convict narrative of Australian literature, Marcus Clarke's *For the Term of His Natural Life (1870-74)* depicts the convict system in terms like those of Mrs. Stowe.[7] While white Australians professed to believe that Aboriginal Australians who lived and worked on the great cattle stations did so voluntarily, Aboriginal Australian people would not willingly leave the territory of their language group because in their culture to do so would be to lose their identity as persons, and rosters of a station's Aboriginal Australian people were part of the legal documents passed from one owner or lessee to another.

While these conditions could be interpreted as validating the claim of the pastoral Squattocracy who favored hierarchical authority and local control, it is also likely that urban workers drew satisfaction from the plays' obvious disapproval of a system in which the workers are both paternalized and powerless. The operation of such a dual appeal is supported by nearly every account of performances through 1880. These plays were performed in the principal theatres at normal prices, and people from all classes attended. After 1880, only the cheapest seats were regularly filled, and performances were increasingly housed in minor theatres at reduced prices, suggesting an appeal limited to those at the bottom of the wage scale.

Moreover, the conventionalized incompetence and docility of the blackface characters could be regarded as justifying both the traditional treatment of Australian Aborigines and the demand for a "White Australia," which increased with the approach of federation. Theatrical blacks seem to have served as surrogates for the threatening hordes of Polynesians and Asians that seemed to imperil the Anglo-Saxon outpost of the Antipodes.

Such attitudes toward groups were not necessarily applied to individuals. There were African and Caribbean blacks among the convicts, and the character of Martin

Beck, a station overseer and central character in Alexander Harris's early Australian novel, *The Emigrant Family* (1849), was apparently based on the person of Tom Britt, a West Indian resident of Goulburn.[8] There are numerous instances of African-Americans being treated as equals in the Australian gold fields, while African-American performers were free of the racial segregation that was common in the United States after the Civil War.[9]

As in Great Britain, Australians had been used to black-face minstrel entertainment long before they read or saw *Uncle Tom's Cabin* (J. S. Bratton; Richard Waterhouse), but the Yankee character was new to them.[10] They encountered him in the context of the Southern slave drama, principally *Uncle Tom's Cabin* and *The Octoroon*. These two plays were the core of the idiomatic American repertory in pre-federation Australia for two performers from opposite ends of the professional spectrum: Joseph Jefferson III, descendent of a family of professional actors and as bright a star as ever swung in the American theatrical heavens, and ex-slave, Hosea Easton.[11]

Joseph Jefferson III

Born into a theatrical family that went back to his great-grandfather, Jefferson was on stage at the age of four. By the early 1850s, he was a respectable stock actor and stage manager in Baltimore and Washington, D.C. In 1857, he accepted an engagement with Laura Keene for her theatre in New York City, and in his second season created the role of Asa Trenchard, the transcendental Yankee of Tom Taylor's *Our American Cousin*. He continued his ascent in Dion Boucicault's company at the Winter Garden where he became the original Salem Scudder, the Yankee overseer of the plantation, in *The Octoroon*.

These successes led him to look for a starring vehicle, which he believed he had found in Washington Irving's story of Rip Van Winkle. Arranging his own stage version from three that already existed (including one by his half-brother Charles Burke), he set out as a star. Coming to San Francisco in 1861, he played from 8 July to 18 August 1861 at Maguire's Opera House. During his stay, he formed a friendship with H. A. Perry, the leading man of the stock company, and his Australian bride, Agnes Land. Perry had played successfully in Australia as had James Stark, McKean Buchanan, and Joey Gougenheim that summer. More importantly, the Civil War had disrupted theatre in the South, increasing competition elsewhere. These would have been among the reasons that prompted Jefferson to sail for Sydney on 10 September 1861.

With the exception of one visit to New Zealand, he played in Australia more or less continuously from 1862 until 1865, domesticating comfortably in Melbourne with a young actress by whom he had a son. If he had not been a widower with children in America, one wonders if he might have stayed as Joey Gougenheim had done, and as Hosea Easton, J. C. Williamson, and Maggie Moore were to do, but when the war ended, he went on to London and epic success, particularly after Boucicault revised his version of the Rip Van Winkle story. Subsequently identified with that role, he became an icon rather than an actor, a force of nature rather than a mere mortal, the equal of Edwin Booth. After retirement, he wrote the most genial actor's autobiography of all time. Even his quarrels and disappointments are bathed in the glow of a generous nature and good fortune.

Unlike Booth, Jefferson was a polished, mature professional when he stepped onto the stage of Sydney's Royal Victoria Theatre as Rip on 3 February 1862. He was a star when he took his farewell at Melbourne's Royal Haymarket as Bob Brierly in Taylor's *The Ticket-of-Leave Man* on 7

March 1865, and it was undoubtedly the process of refining his style for the Anglo-Australian audience that was the basis for his subsequent London success.

He regularly acted eleven main pieces, most frequently Caleb Plummer in Boucicault's adaptation of *Cricket on the Hearth*, Bob Brierly in Taylor's *Ticket-of-Leave Man*, Rip Van Winkle, Asa Trenchard, but most often Salem Scudder in *The Octoroon*. Additionally, his repertory contained nine afterpieces which he offered either in addition to a main piece or with other afterpieces to make an evening's bill. The only classical role in his repertory was Bob Acres in *The Rivals*, and in Melbourne during August and September of 1862, he played Bottom, Dogberry, and Crabtree (*School for Scandal*). However, these forays into the classics were insignificant. Jefferson's strength was as an idiomatic common man in roles which intertwined the comic and the pathetic.

He said that he always prepared a role carefully and in elaborate detail, always listened carefully and tried not to detract from what other actors did, never acknowledged the presence of the audience, and acted best with a warm heart and a cool head. He also advised Otis Skinner to play against comic points: the more absurd the line, the more serious its delivery; the more outrageous the situation or business, the more matter of fact its execution. Most of his Australian reviews support his claims, particularly those of James Smith, for whom Jefferson was the ideal natural actor. To what extent Smith's enthusiastic reviews were responsible for his popularity is unclear, but Jefferson played over three hundred nights in Melbourne, compared to slightly more than a hundred in Sydney and less than sixty in either Adelaide or Hobart.[12]

Jefferson's Asa Trenchard was not defined by his accent, although comments suggest that it was always present, but by the style of his acting. Where Americans were supposed to be boisterous, Jefferson was quiet:

Jefferson displayed his perfectly finished style of acting, making his part natural and effective without descending to the vulgarity and coarseness which, thanks to Mr. Dickens, is associated with our ideas of the Yankee character.

(*Advertiser*, 14 July 1863)

Remembering Jefferson's performance some years later, Dr. Neild provides an insight into his use of comic business to undercut sentiment. As he expressed a deep feeling, "His ready wit suggested an ingeniously opportune diversion—the picking of 'a hank of cotton,' or the lighting a cigar. ...He did not seem to be playing to a crowd of spectators; or, indeed, to anybody at all" (*Australasian*, 21 December 1878). Consequently, as James Smith noted,

There is nothing in all he says or does which could jar upon the most sensitive feeling, or shock the most fastidious taste. Asa Trenchard, as depicted by this gentleman, sins against the conventionalities, but not against the decencies or proprieties of civilised life, and herein consists the feature which distinguishes the accomplished and refined actor from the merely clever buffoon.

(*Age*, 26 April 1862)

The critic in Hobart not only approved of the style but connected the character's good qualities with his national citizenship:

Mr. Jefferson's "Asa Trenchard" is a very different character to the orthodox American of the English stage. It is the real picture of an American gentleman, bred in the school of social freedom, whose every day life and actions have been untrammeled by the ridiculous conventionalities of "polite society."

(*Mercury*, 4 March 1864)

As the critic for the Argus noted, "cousin Jonathan...has been grossly misrepresented, and the worship of the 'almighty dollar' is a fiction. If Asa Trenchard is a type of his countrymen, their best virtues are unknown" (22 April 1862).

While it was his portrait of Asa Trenchard that drew the most fulsome praise in Australia, it was as Salem Scudder that Jefferson most often appeared there. *The Octoroon* offered not only a Yankee character similar to Asa, but also a resonant depiction of slavery. Between 1853 and 1860, there were fewer than a hundred performances of adaptations of Mrs. Stowe's novel in the colonies. By comparison, there were nearly two hundred performances of *The Octoroon* in the 1860s. It was Boucicault's play and Jefferson's performance that created the American South for Australians.

There were two versions of the play. In the original American one, Zoe (the octoroon) commits suicide. This ending aroused a negative reaction when played in London, so Boucicault eliminated it. Jefferson, however, played the original version because it was the one in which he had created Scudder. The play was admired for its accuracy in its depiction of slaves, slavery, and human nature in general. The writer for the *Herald* thought it was particularly effective in displaying on stage both the physical and the economic cruelty of slavery (1 October 1864). However, it was Jefferson's playing that attracted the most comment.

Jefferson was not the first Salem Scudder in Australia, but he was definitive, and later players of the role were always described and evaluated in terms of their likeness to him. Nothing in the notices of earlier performances could have prepared one for the effulgence of praise that greeted Jefferson's Salem Scudder. By far the most elaborate was James Smith:

If we pay Mr. Jefferson a compliment at the expense of his native country, we do not think that any sensible compatriot of his will feel irritated in consequence. We may therefore, at once declare that this gentleman's acting since he has been in Melbourne…has impressed the majority, at least, of those who have witnessed his performance, with a new conception of the character of the people of the United States. …Where is there to be found in any moderate range of the drama a more thoroughly manly, because simple and unaffected hero, than the unpretentious Salem Scudder of this accomplished artist?

(*Age*, 27 May 1862)

The play remained extremely popular with some 350 performances between 1870 and 1880, but its popularity then declined rapidly. *Uncle Tom's Cabin* gradually supplanted it, recording between 225 and 250 performances a decade between 1870 and 1915. Curiously, though, *The Octoroon* was always more popular in Melbourne than in Sydney, while the opposite was true for *Uncle Tom*.

While there were two versions of *The Octoroon*, there were at least ten of *Uncle Tom* performed in Australia. The first performances in Sydney probably used Thomas H. Lacey's adaptation (Theatre Royal, Manchester, 1 February 1853) published by Samuel French. H. J. Conway's was played by Charles Thorne and Kate Denin in 1854. Anna Quinn performed in a version by Frank Fowler, *Eva, or Leaves From Uncle Tom's Cabin* (25 August 1856). The Marsh Juveniles presented George Aiken's adaptation, which was the American standard version (12 May 1862). Aiken's script was probably the basis for the personalized versions claimed by J. C. Williamson (Sydney, 28 June 1875), Carrie Swain (Sydney, 16 May 1887), and Walter Sanford (Sydney, 20 August 1904). However, the longest run was achieved by an Australian version, based on Lacey's, prepared by W. H.

Wallace, stage manager of the Princess's Theatre, Melbourne (8 June to 6 September 1878). Most of these versions retain the deaths of Eva and Tom. However, Conway and two other Australian adaptations omit one or both. Alfred Dampier's omitted Eva's death, and left George and Eliza alive in New Orleans (*Australasian*, 9 August 1879), while George Rignold's allowed Tom to join George and Eliza in Canada rather than being beaten to death at Legree's command (*SMH*, 10 September 1888). Regardless, the newspaper reviews stress the unique combination of pathos and comedy and the antics of Topsy as characteristic of plantation life. The following review is typical:

> The clever admixture of humor and pathos in *"Uncle Tom's Cabin"* may be taken as eminently characteristic of that curious mass of humanity which groaning under the oppression of an iniquitous system of slavery, yet sought relief from the monotony of work and whip in the indulgence of an innate spirit of drollery, which found expression in quaint pastimes and jocund song.
>
> (*Advertiser*, 24 February 1896)

Hosea Easton

Hosea Easton appeared as Uncle Tom in the versions by Aiken, Wallace, Dampier, and Rignold, and his performance became the standard for the title role. He said he was born a slave, and after emancipation served for three years in the navy, after which he moved to Connecticut and pursued a career as a performer. It was there that he must have appropriated the name of Hosea Easton (1798–1837), a free black, who became a Methodist minister in Hartford, Connecticut. He was an abolitionist and the author of a Treatise, in which he argued that there were no inherent differences between Africans and Caucasians. It seems unlikely that a slave owner would bestow such a person's name on a slave child.[13]

According to Ike Simond, "Hosey Easton" was a member of the George Callender's first minstrel company.[14] Starting out in 1872, they traveled across the United States, reaching San Francisco in 1876. Callender's manager, Charles Hicks, persuaded Easton and some others to go with him to the Antipodes.[15] After three months in New Zealand, they began performing at Hobart on 30 July 1877 (*Mercury*, 30 July to 6 August 1877).

Easton remained in Australia, dying in Sydney on 23 June 1899. He was described as "one of the finest banjoists Australia has ever heard" (*Bulletin*, 6 May 1899) whose "fame was world wide" (*Sydney Morning Herald*, 26 June 1899), and whose "talking banjo" routine included comic asides on theology and temperance that delighted the audience (*SMH*, 24 December 1878). In addition to participating in the skits and operatic burlesques that were part of the normal minstrel show, Easton was the first African-American to play Uncle Tom in Australia (8 June 1878) and later increased his repertory with the roles of Uncle Tiff in a dramatization of Mrs. Stowe's *Dred* (2 November 1878), Uncle Pete in *The Octoroon* (8 July 1884), and Caesar Augustus in Oliver Doud Byron's cavalry and Indian farrago, *Across the Continent* (11 August 1890).

As much or more than any single performer, Hosea Easton validated conventional racial attitudes, but he would have done the same in America, and he was much better off in Australia. He could own property, join unions, travel in first class on the railroad, and marry interracially.[16] In terms of overt discrimination, Easton may well have benefited from the egalitarianism of a nation founded by convicts and others from the social underclass, but he certainly found less competition and greater success in his line of work in Australia than he was likely to have found in the United States.

Easton was the paramount Uncle Tom in Australia. He was the Uncle Tom during the longest consecutive run of performances (Princesses' Theatre, Melbourne, 8 June to 6 September 1878). While he played most often in Sydney and Melbourne, he made substantial tours of the country towns in Victoria during 1889[17] and he had long residences in Queensland (August 1890–January 1892) and Western Australia (August 1896–April 1897).

His performances were always reviewed favorably. His first notice as Uncle Tom in Melbourne was that he "acted with great care and naturalness" (*Age*, 10 June 1878). The *Sydney Morning Herald* described him as acting "with great delicacy and care," and while thinking he was "too tall and slight for the popular idea of Uncle Tom's physical proportions," concluded that "his renderings are pleasing and he divested his actions and speech of that ponderosity which some aspirants to the part assume" (14 October 1878). In Adelaide, the reviewer asserted that most of the company "are not such capable actors as many who have assumed the roles," but noted that Easton played "with a realism that evoked the most hearty commendation of the auditory" (*Advertiser*, 23 December 1879). These early reviews are particularly striking because while Tom was played as an old man, Easton was no more than twenty-five. Late in his career, the *Age* commented on how he "happily showed the difference between a real Negro and his burlesque counterparts" (21 April 1894). The *Daily Telegraph* described him as playing "with much feeling, and at the same time without inartistic straining" (16 July 1894), and after his death referred to him as the standard for embodying "so faithfully and with so much pious earnestness the character of the old Negro" (17 November 1902).

Popular and critical approval translated into greater control over his career than he would have had in the

United States. Easton was an independent agent, starring in a tour of *Uncle Tom* through New South Wales and Queensland in 1890. Later, living in Sydney, he alternated acting for George Rignold at Her Majesty's Theatre and appearing as a variety performer at Harry Rickards's Tivoli Theatre. He also had the opportunity to engage from time to time in theatrical management. In 1885, he had his own banjo orchestra in Melbourne. During 1889, he managed a detachment of minstrels who performed in the country towns of Victoria, and the next year he was credited with staging the scenes of plantation life in *The Octoroon* in Brisbane (*Courier*, 5 August 1890). During 1896, he was listed as joint proprietor of a company with James Wilkinson in Western Australia.

Whatever success Easton experienced, his final years were difficult. *The Bulletin* reported in 1899 that he had cancer of the tongue and "has undergone two terrible operations" (6 May). After his funeral, the *Bulletin* reported that "A week prior to his death Mr. W. J. Stent, of the American Banjo Club, applied to all the principal Sydney hospitals for the admission of poor Easton...but was refused" (22 July 1899).

Australian attitudes had changed sharply during Easton's career, and it is possible that toward its end, he experienced at least some of the hatred that exploded nine years later in reaction to black boxer Jack Johnson's winning the heavyweight championship from Canadian Tommy Burns in Sydney.[18] Considering Easton's career, perhaps it is best to remember him as his colleagues did. Led by a brass band, they accompanied his body to its resting place in Waverley Cemetery on a hillside facing the sea, where they erected a headstone that still records their "affectionate memory of our old brother artist Hosea Easton. Deeply regretted by all who knew him."

CHAPTER 6

The American Idiom: Irish and German

REGARDLESS OF THE POPULARITY of Joseph Jefferson III and Hosea Easton, no two people had a greater impact on the Australian stage than James Cassius Williamson and Maggie Moore. He became the dominant manager for the continent, while she remained its most popular performer.

They came from different backgrounds. Williamson began a traditional theatrical apprenticeship during 1861 at the Academy of Music in Milwaukee where he lived. After several other brief engagements, he went to New York City where he was engaged as a member of Wallack's Theatre company in August 1863. He remained with Wallack's until May 1871 when he left for the California Theatre, San Francisco.

From 1851 to 1887, Wallack's was probably the most respected theatre in the United States. Its founder, James William Wallack, had been a leading actor on the London stage, and his son, Lester, maintained the London repertory tradition when he became manager. During his time there, Williamson worked his way up from the smallest speaking parts to featured eccentric comic roles, such as Sir Lucius O'Trigger. Most importantly, he worked with and would have learned from some of the best players then on the American stage.

Williamson's move to San Francisco was a professional advance. He was engaged as the principal eccentric and low comedian for a company that rivaled even Wallack's. For three seasons, he was featured as Touchstone, the First Gravedigger, Verges, Tony Lumpkin, Uncle Tom, and in the Irish melodramas of Dion Boucicault.

Williamson established himself as an audience favorite. The reviewer for the *Alta* noted that from the first he "has succeeded thus far in presenting each character entirely unlike any preceding it, both in manner and make-up" (19 September 1871), and the same critic continued to praise his originality, as in his playing of Verges:

> Mr. Williamson elevated the part of Verges from that of an old imbecile (as usually played when in the hands of a "second old man") to a distinct character—a loquacious, self-sufficient officer, fond of displaying his "little brief authority" but recognizing the necessity also of acknowledging the supremacy of those in power over him.
>
> (29 April 1873)

He also brought Maggie Moore into the company and married her. She was a San Francisco native whose parents had emigrated from Ireland by way of Australia. Her training was as a singer and dancer in the variety theatres of the city's Barbary Coast. While just as demanding, they were the opposite of Wallack's. Small theatres catering to male audiences, their evening's entertainment included a minstrel show followed by a two- or three-act burlesque drama, the content of which was often impolite. Jefferson De Angelis remembered Gilbert's Melodeon, where his father was a member of the company, as a hall above Ryder and Brennan's saloon with a stage eighteen inches above the floor from which "a tall man could almost reach up and touch the flies." He also remembered that performers had to develop new material weekly to satisfy the regular customers.[1]

Between 1868 and 1872, Maggie Moore and her brother James were billed as "San Francisco Favorites," and appeared on stage regularly singing ballads and dancing numbers such as "The Skipping Rope Hornpipe" and "The Barn Door Jig." She also appeared in small roles supporting stars such as Amy Stone. By October 1870, she was in the company at Thomas Maguire's Metropolitan Theatre where Williamson saw her. That autumn, she made her debut at the California Theatre as Judy O'Trot in the farce *Ireland as it Was*, opposite Williamson as Ragged Pat (28 October 1872). The *Alta* greeted her arrival in momentous terms:

> Miss Maggie Moore has long been recognized as possessed of great talent, more than any of the stars she has so often been called upon to support, but her style needed just that trifle of polish or finish she is now in a fair way to acquire by association with the elite of the profession in a well disciplined company. At the end of her year's engagement...she need not hesitate to travel as a star anywhere.
>
> (29 October 1872)

They were married on 2 February 1873 by Archbishop Alemany at his residence with theatre manager and star John McCullough as best man.

While Williamson performed regularly, Moore was not featured until the holiday season. She played the title role in the pantomime *Aladdin* ("a jovial, good-natured Chinese boy" according to the *Alta* of 26 December) and later as the title role in Burnand's burlesque extravaganza, *Ixion*. Her first real popularity came as Topsy, "She played...with an evident love for the fun of the part, and danced and sang con amore" (*Alta*, 9 June 1873).

For his benefit a few nights later, they appeared as Josephine and as Sgt. Scalade, respectively, in *The Child of the Regiment*, followed by *The Chinese Invasion*, a farce hurriedly written by Clay M. Greene to Williamson's commission. As a pair of Irish servants who are sacked by their master, they contrive to be rehired in the guise of a Chinese couple. They wreak so much havoc that their employer is only too happy to have them back in their true identities. The piece used the xenophobia then current in California as an excuse for slapstick humor. While the audience laughed, the *Alta* was not amused. It thought the farce "A mistake as a play, in appealing to the prejudices of a portion of the audience" (16 April 1873) and on its front page reprinted the text of a sermon by Rev. Dr. A. L. Stone, pastor, First Congregational Church, urging Christian tolerance.

The next season peaked early in 1874 when they supported Dion Boucicault in a round of his own plays. He, of course, played the leads, roles that Williamson would otherwise have played. Williamson played the second male parts, and Moore, surprisingly, played the heroines, completing the transition from variety artist to actress. It seems clear that Boucicault had an important influence on both of them as an acting coach. The *Alta* noted that under Boucicault's direction, Williamson played both Danny Mann (*Colleen Bawn*) and Michael Feeney (*Arrah-na-Pogue*) in new and different ways—not all of which it thought effective (23 and 27 January 1874). However, the critic fully approved of Moore's playing. As Kate Desmond in *Kerry* she showed, "A wider range of action than in the parts she has heretofore played. Her Kate was subdued and ladylike throughout" (*Alta*, 20 January 1874), while as Arrah she, "Fully identified herself with the exquisite creation" (*Alta*, 27 January 1874).

Actors who achieved this kind of success in such a theatre in the United States had nowhere to go except on the road as stars. What they needed was a vehicle. Their talent was not suited to the standard repertory. They were comic specialists, and Williams again resorted to Clay Greene, who gives this account:

A lumber man, Samuel W. Smith, to relieve the winter monotony of his trade by attempts at playwriting, had written a short drama in two scenes, dealing with the adventures of a stupid Pennsylvania Dutchman as a raw recruit in the American Civil war, and ending with the discovery of oil on his farm.

When my work on this commission was completed, Williamson unreservedly accepted it and produced it shortly afterwards in Salt Lake City under the title of *Struck Oil*. Its success there led to its production at the California Theatre, where its reception led to its adoption by the Williamsons as the one feature of a projected starring tour to Australia.[2]

Their Utah try-out as John Stofel and his daughter Lizzie came in the second half of February, and the San Francisco premiere was on 31 March. The *Alta* thought that "Mr. Williamson has got such a play as he needs to star with, and he will probably make a fortune" (1 April 1874), an opinion echoed by others, including Andrew Birrell, the San Francisco agent for Melbourne manager George Coppin.[3] All that remained was to embark on their first tour, which they did, leaving San Francisco for Australia on 27 May 1874.

They arrived in Sydney on 1 July after a voyage in a ship so dirty that Maggie Moore later wrote, "The great big cockroaches carried her along" (Moore).[4] On 4 July, they left for Melbourne and opened at Coppin's Theatre Royal in *Struck Oil*. Dr. Neild wrote:

> Mr. Williamson's acting is easy, unforced, and...natural. ...He never forces his opportunities. ...His accent is so complete as never to suggest that it is, after all, an Englishman trying to speak broken English.
>
> (*Australasian*, 8 August 1874)

Similarly, he thought Moore's acting was distinguished by "a total absence of affectation, and yet it is quite as entirely free from over-demonstrativeness." James Smith added an additional note of analytical praise: "The lady is especially remarkable in that she is able to sustain eccentric parts of a kind not commonly affected by actresses" (*Argus*, 3 August 1874).

They played the colonies until 2 October 1875 in a repertory that included Boucicault's *Kerry*, John Brougham's *Little Nell and the Marchioness*, and Williamson's own version of *Rip Van Winkle*, but they lived on *Struck Oil* (127 performances). The reviewers found weaknesses in some of Williamson's portrayals. The *Age* reviewer faulted them in *Little Nell and the Marchioness*: "Miss Moore's expressions of sentiment are not to be compared with her delineations of the ludicrous. ...Mr Williamson gave a very clever rendering. ...It was, however, an Americanised Dick Swiveller, and depicted the New York...type" (19 October 1874).

It was a different matter when they appeared as John and Lizzie. The play's run of forty-three nights in Melbourne was the longest in the colonies up to that time, and their share of the receipts exceeded $2,000 a week.[5] In Sydney, the *Herald* thought the combination of Williamson and Moore in *Struck Oil*, "One of the most thrilling dramas, and some of the most accomplished performers that have come before a Sydney audience for many years. ...Williamson's rendition of John Stofel...[is] fully equal...to Mr. Jefferson's Rip Van Winkle" (10 March 1875). In Adelaide, the *Advertiser* preferred the character of Stofel to that of Rip because he was neither drunk nor lazy (30 August 1875). Comparisons with Jefferson were inevitable, and most opinions echoed Dr. Neild's description of the difference between the two. Williamson's humor, "bubbles, and ripples, and sparkles...it does not lurk in deep shady pools, and suddenly dash over big boulders…but it goes with a sort of jaunty flow" (*Australasian*, 21 November 1874).

The Williamsons left Australia having netted $75,000 for their efforts.[6] The festivities attending the Prince of Wales's visit to India provided an opportunity for two weeks of *Struck Oil* in Calcutta, followed by a brief season in Bombay on their way to London.[7] Beginning on Easter Monday (17 April 1876), they played at the Adelphi Theatre until 12 August. Most of the run was of an astonishing double bill that paired *The Colleen Bawn* with *Struck Oil*, after which they revived *Arrah-na-Pogue*. Returning to San Francisco, they revived *Struck Oil*, and the *Alta* noted that the play "has been so thoroughly revised, improved, built upon and cut since its first production in San Francisco that little is left of the original save the skeleton" (10 July 1877). Clay Greene agreed, and Williamson's regular royalty payments to him ceased. Greene did, however, resign his seat on the San Francisco stock exchange to become the Williamson's business manager for their American tour which lasted (with summer interruptions) until the spring of 1879.

When they returned to Australia that July, they were equipped both with old favorites and new delights, the Australian rights to Gilbert and Sullivan's *H. M. S. Pinafore*. When that proved successful, Williamson acquired the rights to *The Pirates of Penzance* and *Patience*. They played steadily throughout Australia and New Zealand for the next four years. While *Struck Oil* remained the piece they played most often (over 150 times), the comic operas combined for over 250. In *Pinafore*, Moore at first played Josephine, but came gradually to specialize in Little Buttercup. In *Penzance,* she was Ruth, while in *Patience,* she appeared as Lady Jane. Williamson played Sir Joseph Porter and the Sergeant of Police in the first two pieces, respectively, and did not appear in the third. Moore's reception was always favorable, while Williamson's was guarded. The following comments about *Pinafore* from the *Advertiser* are typical: Moore "sang in a style that would not disgrace a prima donna, and played with an archness that was quite in keeping with the character"; but of Williamson, it said, "Fortunately for himself he has not a great deal of singing to do, although he gave his principal song quite creditably, but was astray in a bit of recitative in the second act" (11 May 1880).

From 1883 through 1888, they played shorter seasons, introducing new plays, but Williamson became more and more occupied with management. Much of his time was spent defending his rights. There was no firm precedent for recognizing English copyright in Australia, and the issue had to be litigated in each colony.[8] His growing involvement in business led him to become lessee of Melbourne's Theatre Royal in 1881 and enter into various partnerships with other managers and producers. He stopped playing at the end of 1888, appearing on stage thereafter only on a handful of special occasions. Maggie Moore stopped as well, but their further careers are part of another chapter.

They were actors of opposite strategies. Williamson was a character actor. By means of costume, make-up, speech, posture, and gesture, he seems to have created a different stage persona for each character. She seems to have done the opposite. Regardless of costume or dialect, she was the same in every role. She presented a generic persona which the audience understood to be an extension of her own personality. In spite of their different methods, both were accepted with equal fervor. The combination of their two different approaches seemed to please the audience. Perhaps that is because, like Jefferson, they were both absorptive players. By different means, they made the inner lives of their characters present to the audience. Playing as though the audience was not present, they invited its members to join them in living the fiction.

By whatever means, they played many characters. Other dialect players usually played only a single character, and their more limited success reinforces the significance of Williamson's and Moore's achievement. Between 1876 and 1880 the colonies were visited by Joseph K. Emmet and the team of Peter F. Baker and T. J. Farron. Emmet was the premier German comic on the American stage. Beginning as a variety performer and minstrel in St. Louis, he made his way to New York City by 1868. With Charles Gaylor, he wrote his first starring vehicle, *Fritz, Our Cousin German*, which he first played in Buffalo in 1869 and was supported by Williamson in New York City during the summer of 1870. He followed it with six more vehicles for *Fritz*. Possessing a strong tenor voice, he wrote his own songs and accompanied himself on drums, banjo, and harmonica.

He played Melbourne, Sydney, and Adelaide (with a tour of New Zealand) between 18 March 1876 and 24 July 1877. The papers admired his skill, deplored his material, and acknowledged his popularity. However, his eccentric personal habits were commented on as often as his abilities. Dr. Neild thought he was drunk while performing, and W.H. Ford says he was:

> After a few nights the attendance...fell off very great. ...Joe had taken to drink to drown his disappointment. ...In one scene [he] got so sleepy that he...sank into a chair, laid his arms & head on the table and went to sleep. The audience, including the Governor had to be dismissed and given back their money.[9]

Between 1 July 1876 and 10 January 1880, the team of Peter F. Baker and T. J. Farron toured successfully in their repertory of Dutch specialties: *Conrad and Lizette; or Life on the Mississippi*; *Lisa Eccles*, *The Governor*, *The Cut Glove*, and *Struck Oil*. Baker played the male leads (such as Conrad

Schultzerhooltzdoffin), while Farron doubled German girls and Irish men (Lizette Von Wolfstein/Tim Flaterty).

The *Age* noted that "the entertainment proved to consist mainly of music-hall songs, dutch business, and break-downs" (2 October 1876), and wondered "why people should pay to see but poorly acted on the stage what they can see for nothing acted to the life any night in the streets and slums of the town" (23 October 1876). Whatever the critic's reservations, the audiences were enthusiastic. The *Town and Country Journal* (Sydney) reported that "nothing could exceed the vehement shouting and applause with which their most trivial acts were received" (8 July 1876), and the *Mercury* thought, "We have never seen in this city an assembly so convulsive with incessant laughter as that which nearly filled the theatre last night" (21 November 1876). However, the paper did think, "There are parts in the burlesque...that are too broad, and not likely to please an assemblage of ladies and gentlemen" (28 November 1876).

In spite of his previous disapproval, the critic of the *Age* liked them in *Struck Oil*, "Mr. Baker played his part...with that fidelity which comes of long practice and intimate association with original John Stofels," and he compared Farron favorably to Maggie Moore (7 January 1878). In Adelaide, the *Advertiser* went farther in making a direct comparison:

> Baker's John Stofel...is much weaker, less pathetic, and not so genuinely humorous though more boisterously funny than Williamson's. ...Farron is more artistic than was Maggie Moore, and does not offend the proprieties by standing with his back to the audience for several minutes as she did while singing her farewell to the old man who is called away to war.
>
> (10 June 1879)

How they came by their text of *Struck Oil* is unknown, but as they were leaving, they sold it to MacLean's Dramatic Troubadours, a company of children. By then, however, Williamson had returned and gone to court to stop them. He even got a published apology from Baker and Farron.

Playing Irish characters, of course, had been a specialty of both Gustavus Vaughn Brooke and Barry Sullivan, but they had not done so exclusively. Grattan Riggs and John F. Sheridan played Irish parts almost without exception. Riggs had been a variety performer in New York in the early 1860s. By 1877, he had written *The Irish Detective*, which sustained him for the rest of his career. As a detective, he was called upon to disguise himself as an Englishman, a German, an African-American, an Irish man, and an Irish woman. Dr. Neild summed him up as "a genial, pleasant, cheery actor. …Like every other stage Irishman, there is a good deal of the artificial and the traditional in his representation; but…that appears to be inevitable" (*Australasian*, 3 April 1880).

Sheridan began as part of the clog dancing partnership of Sheridan and Mack in New York City at the end of the Civil War, and by 1880, had found his life's role as the Widow Bridget O'Brien in the burlesque *Fun on the Bristol*. He was in Australia from 1884 until 1892, returning in 1899 and remaining until his death. As the *Age* remarked:

> It mattered very little…under what particular feminine cognomen Mr. Sheridan was masquerading. …[There is] very little plot and what there is takes place in the first act. The last half is merely a setting for a…programme of songs and other items.
>
> (24 February 1902)

But he was well-liked and genuinely mourned. In his obituary, the *Herald* remembered his "ceaseless activity, light-hearted nature, and unfailing kindness" (2 January 1909).

James and Julia Polk also figure in this discussion because they played both Yankees and Hebrews (a sub-class of the German or Dutch idiom). As a young actor, James had been a contemporary of Williamson's in Wallack's company and had acted for Augustin Daly before establishing himself as a light and eccentric comedian with A. M. Palmer's Union Square Company. A lyric soprano, Julia Parker married Polk in 1867, and by 1880, they had begun to tour as stars in vehicles written for them. They played Australia and New Zealand from 30 September 1882 through 29 May 1884. Of his portrayal of the title character in *Sam'l of Posen*, the *Age* wrote:

> Mr. Polk...portrayed a Hebrew of a class altogether different from what is usually seen upon the stage. It was a fine piece of character acting, quiet and natural. ...The actor altogether sank his identity and his dialect.
>
> (6 November 1882)

The Polks returned to the United States where they continued to play successfully until well into the 1890s.

Given the continued appeal of *Struck Oil*, one is tempted to consider its possible connections with Australians, just as one did with *Uncle Tom's Cabin* and *The Octoroon*. Since the play has never been printed, a brief summary is necessary. John Stofel is a German immigrant shoemaker who lives in rural Pennsylvania with his daughter, Lizzie, and his second wife, Katrina. As German natives, both John and Lizzie speak comic English and are frequent sources of laughter for their failure to understand the customs of their new country. Like Rip Van Winkle, John is lazy and, at least until he married Katrina, a drinker. However, he understands economic gain. When the local church deacon, Eben Skinner, is drafted to fight in the Civil War, he turns to John as his replacement. Stofel drives a hard bargain, getting $200 and the deed to a good farm. Without telling Katrina or Lizzie, he hides the deed behind a loose brick in the chimney and goes off to war. The second act is a burlesque of military manners in which John does everything wrong. It is a series of comic bits of business for the actor playing Stofel. The story resumes in the third act. The war has been over for five years. Lizzie, now speaking almost perfect English, has married sweetheart Billy, now Dr. Brown. They know that John had been wounded in the head during the war, but no one has seen him since, and they presume him dead. This opens the way for Skinner, who denies giving the farm to Stofel, to buy John's shop from Katrina. Skinner knows that it sits atop a valuable oil deposit. Just as the deed is about to be consummated, Stofel wanders in unrecognized, and recovers his wits and his memory as the result of an operation performed by Dr. Brown. He retrieves the deed to the farm, and Skinner is arrested for fraud as the curtain falls on the reunited family.[10]

Once again, the appeals were many and simultaneous. To begin with, there is the comic appeal of the immigrant father and daughter. In the United States, German or "Dutch" (Deutsche) characters emerged as a result of the large-scale immigration following the crushing of the revolutionary movement of 1848. The comic German became as much of a commonplace as the Yankee or the Irish and found its foremost literary expression in the ballads of "Hans Breitmann," written by Charles G. Leland and published between 1868 and 1870, around the time Williamson was moving to San Francisco.

However, the specific parody of Germans, like that of the Irish, is merely a strategy for creating a basic form of humor. Much of what the immigrant characters say and do is broadly funny. Their dialogue is a web of puns and malapropisms. In addition, Lizzie is an inveterate practical joker; she is what Australians would call a "larrikin." Moreover, she is constantly breaking into song and dances. Not only are John and Lizzie funny in their own right, but they are vehicles of satire directed against those with money and power. By themselves, these would be powerful appeals to working class members of the audience.

Beyond this, however, the Stofel family is domestically virtuous. While a larrikin, Lizzie loves her father and her stepmother, and Katrina returns the affection. This appeal to the middle-class ideal of domestic harmony is reinforced by Stofel's willingness to risk his life in order to own a farm of his own. Such a desire would have particular appeal in Australia. Most of the best agricultural land was owned by a small number of people, and a series of land reform acts of the 1860s had failed to change that. The mass of colonists were shut out of land ownership and resented the fact. By contrast to Australia, America was a place where the average person, who would soon be stereotyped as the "Aussie Battler" in the fiction of Steele Rudd, could get and keep enough land to support his family. One ought not to overlook these social and economic appeals of a story that seems, on the surface, to be nothing more than a vehicle for comic versatility. Dr. Neild was being perfectly serious when he referred to it as "a good acting domestic drama" (*Australasian*, 12 January 1878).

CHAPTER 7

Cultural Transition, 1880–1915

IN 1880, AUSTRALIA WAS A COUNTRY but not a nation. Each of its six colonies had its own legislature, as well as its own laws and tariffs; and while they all used British currency and sang "God Save the Queen," what truly united them was a common aspiration of the native-born middle class to rise from the status of colonies to that of provinces. In spite of geography, they strove to become home counties rather than foreign dominions. This was the period during which they accomplished their goal. English visitors described Australia as a piece of England. They compared Australia's cities to British provincial ones and stressed the familiar names of streets and suburbs, the brands of goods in the shops, the dress and manners of the inhabitants. Finally, the celebrations of Australia's centenary and Victoria's jubilee seemed to confirm the success of the effort to achieve provincial status.

At the same time, they were increasingly aware that they were in the process of becoming something else—a nation with interests different from the mother country. The traditional view of Australia as a part of Great Britain was usually associated with pastoralists and the middle class, while the newer perception of Australia as a different country was more common among the working class. However, these ideas cut across class divisions as different responses to the same changes.

The most important were the growth of the population and its closer connection to Europe. The population of Australia more than doubled between 1860 and 1900, from 1.145 million to 3.765 million. By 1900, New South Wales was the largest colony (1.6 million), followed closely by Victoria (1.2 million). By 1900, Sydney was slightly larger than Melbourne, each with more than half a million inhabitants. Queensland became the third largest colony, followed by South Australia, while because of the gold rush of 1897, Western Australia drew abreast of Tasmania.[1] In all colonies, about one-third of the people lived in the principal city. They were overwhelmingly Anglo-Celtic, and more than three-quarters of them had been born in Australia. Most importantly, the ratio of men to women went from 1.5 to 1.1.[2]

This larger, native-born population with approximately equal numbers of men and women was much less isolated than its ancestors had been. First, they were less isolated from each other. Telegraph connections between capital cities were accomplished by 1877.[3] While various track gauges were used, railroad mileage increased from 340 in 1860 to 10,500 in 1900,[4] and during the 1880s, New South Wales, Victoria, Queensland, and South Australia were all connected by rail.[5] An ironic example of the change was the manner in which Ned Kelly, the last of the bushrangers, was captured in 1880. Police were notified by telegraph of his presence in Glenrowan, and they arrived there by train.[6]

Australians were also much less isolated from the rest of the world. The submarine telegraph cable connected the continent to Europe by way of India in 1872, meaning that news arrived within forty-eight hours rather than in six or eight weeks. The opening of the Suez Canal in 1879 meant that mail steamers arrived once a week rather than once a month, and the voyage to England was reduced from three months to five weeks. Moreover, the canal meant that

French and German passenger ships began stopping at Australian ports, increasing options for travel to and from Europe.[7]

Increasing population and decreasing distance stimulated the economy. Australians lived off the raw materials provided by their land. Wool was the most important export. While the price fell from a shilling to eight-and-half-pence per pound, the quantity increased so that the value of wool exports doubled between 1860 and 1900.[8] There were also major mineral finds: silver, lead, and zinc at Broken Hill in western New South Wales in 1883, and gold at Kalgoorlie, Western Australia, in 1897. Housing boomed, and by 1900, 40 percent of Australians lived in housing they either owned or were purchasing on a mortgage.

However, half the capital invested between 1860 and 1890 came from English and Scottish banks, and more than half the profits were paid to persons not living in Australia. London's Barings Bank had failed in November 1890, which led to massive withdrawals of capital from Australia, and by May 1892, thirteen of the twenty-two largest Australian banks had closed. Prices for sheep and wheat fell by 50 percent. Then drought set in from 1895 to 1903. Emigration to Australia stopped, along with most economic activity, plunging Australia into a depression and a period of labor unrest that was exacerbated by the inefficiencies of differing railroad gauges and internal tariffs between colonies.[9] There had been a maritime strike in 1890, but the violence of the shearer's strike on Queensland's Barcaldene Downs in 1891 and the miner's strike at Broken Hill the following year seemed to herald revolution reminiscent of Eureka Stockade. The one bright spot was the gold rush around Kalgoorlie in Western Australia, which drew hordes of Victoria's unemployed and turned Perth from a country town to an instant city.[10]

It seemed clear to political leaders such as Henry Parkes, Edmund Barton, and George Reid of New South Wales and Alfred Deakin of Victoria, that the federation of the colonies into a single commonwealth would help remedy the depression. However, federation, suggested as early as 1846 by Colonial Secretary Lord Earl Grey, was seen as doing much more than that because of developments in the way Australians thought of themselves that became clear in the 1880s and dominated until the First World War. As independent, self-governing, voluntary members of the Empire, Australians felt a renewed attachment to their British heritage that found its ultimate expression in the contribution of soldiers to both the Boer War and the First World War.

The Great Britain to which Australians renewed their cultural and political loyalty was itself changing. As the century drew to a close, Britons experienced a sense of decline. The mood shifted from Tennyson's optimism, "To strive, to seek, to find, and not to yield" (*Ulysses*) to Kipling's nostalgia, "Lest we forget—lest we forget" (*Recessional*). Victoria's death and political developments in the new century seemed to confirm the sense of decline and ending. The Tories, the party of the landed aristocracy, were voted out, and the government of middle-class Liberals seemed ineffective. With the crossing of the traditional ruling class to the opposition benches in Parliament, the traditional fabric of society seemed to tear open. It was clear that the plight of the working classes had worsened during the Victorian era. There were many more poor, and they were much worse off. Workers were striking with greater frequency and violence, and an independent Labour Party emerged. Women seemed determined to renounce their traditional roles as wives and mothers as they agitated for birth control, divorce, and the vote. There was great fear that all these liberating forces would combine to substitute passion for reason and individual will for established institutions of order.[11]

Increasingly, the native-born Australian population saw itself as a group with interests that were distinct and different from the views of those who lived at "home" in Great Britain. They saw themselves as a special community that needed protection against outside influence. This view can be illustrated both in the conduct of foreign affairs and in the emergence of an Australian national type in literature.

Australians had always depended on Great Britain for defense. Australians who volunteered for military service in the Sudan (1885), South Africa (1899–1902), China (1900), and the First World War (1914–1918) became members of the British army, commanded by British officers. Yet during the last decades of the nineteenth century, Australians began to fear that British foreign policy interests were not the same as their own. Perhaps because their continent had been free of war, Australians always feared the spread of European conflict to the Pacific. Primarily concerned with Europe, India, and Africa, Great Britain took a relatively sanguine view of foreign expansion in the Pacific. By contrast, Australians were alarmed by Germany's claim of control over northern New Guinea, by the Japanese military success during the Russo-Japanese War (1904–1905), and by short-term success of the Boxer Rebellion against foreign influence in China (1912). This concern was intensified by the difficulty in subduing the rebels in the Boer War (1899–1902), which suggested that British military might was no longer supreme. The difference in point of view was so great that, in 1883, Queensland annexed the island of New Guinea as a defensive measure against German expansion. The action was quashed by the Home Office, only reinforcing the perception that while Australians might have confidence in the British military, they had reason to question the British politicians.

This perception of separate interests was part of a growing awareness of just how different Australians were from their European cousins. A chronic shortage of labor meant that Australians could afford to be independent in their attitude. There was ample work, high wages, a low cost of living, and a mild climate.[12] They did not fear their employers, and by 1890, they controlled the colonial governments and professions. They practiced a public equality of manner, regardless of wealth:

> The lower middle-class and the upper middle-class are much less distinct than at home, and come more freely and frequently…into contact with each other. The distribution of wealth is far more equal. To begin with, there is no poor class in the colonies. Comfortable incomes are in the majority, millionaires few and far between.[13]

The only group considered elite were those who maintained the closest, strongest connections with Great Britain, reading British papers, visiting regularly, and sending their sons to school there. At least one English visitor, Percy F. Rowland, thought that such class distinctions as he observed in Australia were almost inversely disproportionate to the actual class differences.[14]

During the 1880s, popular literature coalesced around the mythic figure of the Australian bushman who was the equivalent of the American frontiersman. Although most Australians lived in cities and suburbs, their economy depended on the activity of the rural minority of miners, selectors, shepherds, shearers, and jackaroos (workers on sheep and cattle stations). This emerging character combined the attitudes of convicts, larrikins, and bushrangers as Australians combined the rebellion at the Eureka Stockade with the shearers strike on the Barcaldene Downs.

The bushman worked for wages and never expected any better. He was literate, practical, and inventive, stoically coping with hardship and enduring disaster. Egalitarian by choice, communitarian by necessity, laconic by temperament, he was as ready to mock himself or his mate as he was to share his last ration of water and damper with a passing stranger. Both subject and reader of the poems and stories written by A. B. "Banjo" Patterson, Henry Lawson, and scores of other contributors to Sydney's weekly *Bulletin*, he humped his swag across the dusty landscape of the back of beyond, representing those values which set Australians apart from the Englishmen. These differences were reinforced by the painting of the Heidelberg school (Tom Roberts, Arthur Streeton, Frederick McCubbin), who were the first to render the landscape as recognizably Australian rather than as a recreation of the Lake Country.

These changes to the Australian imaginative outlook meant a change in their view of America, and that change affected both the popular and elite repertories. Australians understood that some American national interests were more like their own, and just as many a digger had imitated Yankee behavior on the gold fields, many now saw similarities between their popular hero and the mythic inhabitants of the trans-Mississippi American West.[15] Not only did the landscape of the American West resemble Australia's interior, but American farm machinery was sturdier and better adapted to Australian conditions than the British equivalents.[16] Commenting on American influence in Australia, one British observer noted:

> Americans are succeeding to-day largely because of their climate, their superior education, their longer working hours, their willingness to receive new ideas, their better plant, and perhaps most of all, because of their freedom from hampering traditions.[17]

The accepted view was that because they were a younger civilization, the Americans had more energy and vigor than the British. A sympathetic British commentator, widely read in Australia, James Bryce, observed that:

> They are a hopeful people. Whether or no they are right in calling themselves a new people, they certainly seem to feel in their veins the bounding pulse of youth. They see a long vista of years stretching out before them, in which they will have time enough to cure all their faults, to overcome all obstacles that block their path.[18]

As Barbara Tuchman has observed, Americans believed in the virtue of being self-made, and regarded those who inherited wealth with suspicion.[19]

As if in response to these observations, the United States showed not only a vigor in its domestic economy, but a new assertiveness in foreign affairs. The war with Spain resulted in the United States acquiring the territories of Cuba, Puerto Rico, the Philippines, and Hawaii. To Australians, a vigorous American presence in the Pacific was a welcome antidote to fears about possible invasion by Russians, Germans, or Japanese, and the visit of the American Pacific Fleet in 1908 resulted in a celebration of what Australians took to be the support of the United States for its culture. Australians were impressed not only by the warships but by the behavior of the sailors on shore, and the cultural affinity of the two nations was celebrated in a popular song, "We've Got a Big Brother in America."[20]

American actors and plays began to be more popular in the 1890s and positively flourished in the first decade of the new century. The rise in popularity seems to have begun in 1896 according to the *Dramatic Mirror* (1 August 1896:12), while in the same year the *Bulletin* noted a decided shift of Australian culture away from the British (20 June 1896). Visiting Australia in 1895, Mark Twain noted that Sydney and Melbourne seemed to him like American cities, and he claimed to find no great difference between Australian and American speech and accents.[21]

A growing community of national interests was encouraged by the rise of theatrical monopolies in both countries. In the United States, first-class theatrical productions were largely controlled by the booking firm of Klaw and Erlanger after 1896, while J. C. Williamson with his various partners exerted a similar influence in Australia. Williamson seems to have worked closely with Klaw and Erlanger and with America's most ambitious and successful producer, Charles Frohman, who was active in both New York City and London. An indication of closer coordination between the two countries is the fact that Williamson visited the United States to see productions in 1901 for the first time in six years (*Herald*, 2 February 1901). *The Mirror*'s Australian correspondent (a Williamson employee) repeatedly attributed the success of American plays and players to Williamson's efforts (29 August 1903; 25 June 1904), while the *Bulletin* attributed to "one prominent, popular, and experienced theatrical manager here," the fear that Australian theatricals would be taken over by an American "shindykit" (26 May 1900:8). The following chapters describe those American players and plays that were the primary agents of this theatrical change.

CHAPTER 8

The Elite Repertory after 1880, Part One: Meeting Expectations

AMERICANS PLAYING THE TRADITIONAL REPERTORY did not find the same success during the 1860s and 1870s as their predecessors had. This was because they were mostly ordinary stock actors, while the English competition was much better. Provincial English players of merit steadily occupied the center of the Australian stage after 1860. They offered a particular blend of stylistic qualities popular in the British provinces, combining the Kemble voice and manner of speaking with Macready's more physical action. It was a robust style depending on strong voice, proper elocution, and vigorous but graceful action.[1]

Gustavus Vaughn Brooke, resident from 1855 to 1861, was most admired for his Othello, but respected for Shylock, Richard III, and Macbeth, Richelieu, and Virginius. However, he was equally popular for his comic turns in *His Last Legs*, *The Serious Family*, and *The Lady of Lyons*. He was clearly a follower of Edmund Kean rather than John Phillip Kemble. His acting was robust and larger than life, but he spoke the language musically, managing a conversational clarity within the formal patterns of both verse and prose. He was followed by another provincial Irish player from 1862 to 1866, Barry Sullivan. More gentlemanly, Sullivan was preferred to Brooke as Hamlet and as Charles Surface, and he was a more meticulous producer. The scenery, costumes, and supporting players in Sullivan's productions were generally the best Australians had seen. Still, he played in the same robust style which carried him through a long career. Bernard Shaw described Sullivan as "the very incarnation of the old individualistic, tyrannical conception of a great actor" and noted that both he and Macready "relied for their stage climaxes on effects of violence and impetuosity, and for their ordinary impressiveness on a grandiose assumption of style."[2] Other visiting players of this style popular in Australia at the time were Charles Dillon, Clarence Holt, and James Anderson; and Alfred Dampier settled in Australia in 1873 and continued acting until 1905. Other British actors who settled in Australia during this time were William Hoskins, and the brothers Charles and W. J. Holloway.

Although they clearly preferred the older tradition of acting, Australians were not immune to innovation. The young British tragedian Walter Montgomery brought the blond, softer spoken, more calculating Hamlet of Charles Fechter to the colonies between 1867 and 1869. The contrast between his Hamlet and that of the more traditional Anderson (1867–1868) was stark. Montgomery was unusually quiet, substituting intensity for volume. His Hamlet was an intellectually subtle, emotionally vulnerable young man who went mad as a consequence of emotional trauma, attempting to pass off his breakdown as a deliberate strategy. Anderson was a Hamlet of powerful will, carrying out a series of charades in order to arrive at the revenge demanded by the ghost of his father. Long opposed to the traditional Hamlet, James Neild championed Montgomery, but Anderson was popular and had his defender in James Smith. The two most influential Australian critics contended with each other in the press.[3]

Finally, one must note the visit during 1863–1864 of Charles and Ellen Kean. It did not matter that he was old and in poor health, or that he had never been the dominant actor his father had been. They were the first established London stars to visit Australia. Their performances became rituals of cultural appropriation. It did not matter what they did—indeed their rather low-key style was an acquired taste—as long as they did it in Melbourne and Sydney. Charles Mathews had a similar reception when he appeared in his light comic repertory during 1870–71.

Male actors dominated the repertory, but there were excellent English actresses who came to Australia in this same period. The best liked was Fanny Cathcart, who was Brooke's leading lady, and who, between 1855 and 1877, starred opposite both her first husband, Robert Heir, and her second, George Darrell. She was most frequently compared to Louisa Cleveland (Mrs. Charles Vincent), who began acting in Australia in 1865. Neild's opinion seemed generally accepted that while Cathcart was the best all-round actress, Cleveland had greater emotional depth.[4]

In this context, American actors had a far more difficult time finding critical or popular favor than had their predecessors. It was not sufficient to be capable; one had to be distinctive. Among the men, James Carden, Charles Pope, and George D. Chaplin were sturdy journeymen, while Edwin Adams's visit was cut short by illness. The women—May Howard, Jane Coombs, and Annie Pixley— were ambitious ingenues.

The situation changed during the 1880s. Although it has been characterized as a decade of decline for the performance of Shakespeare in Australia, the number of his plays produced remained constant, and the number of performances increased slightly over the previous decade. The sense of decline was more of quality than quantity. The decade saw few significant British actors and limited innovation. Among resident actors, Alfred Dampier remained faithful to the style of Brooke, season after season, inserting performances of *Hamlet, Othello, The Merchant of Venice, Romeo and Juliet,* and *As You Like It* into long runs of popular melodramas, while the two most significant British visitors were George Rignold and the duo of W. J. Holloway and his stepdaughter Essie Jenyns.

The Americans who presented the classical repertory in Australia after 1880 were all young, but they came from different backgrounds that reflected the shifting trends in American theatre. It was primarily their youth and generally more subdued, absorptive style that recommended them. At the same time, the plays of Shakespeare provided one of the most significant connections with the culture of England, and the style of their performance was a crucial element in the middle class's appropriation of identity.

Because of the size and distribution of its population, the United States supported a universe of successful provincial actors who developed styles popular with regional audiences. Thus, although New York City was the capital of American theatricals, there was much greater provincial independence than in England or Australia. The result was a range of styles as large and expansive as the nation itself, not only vocally and physically more exaggerated than its British counterpart, but also favoring individuality of interpretation in line reading and stage business. Since the Civil War, however, the style had undergone a slow process of refinement as the American middle class dominated the Gilded Age. An inner concentration, expressed by vocal understatement and significant silences, by physical pose and tableaux, and typified in the acting of Edwin Booth, began to replace vocal and physical exaggeration as signs of emotional intensity and psychological truth.[5]

Such acceptability involved both the kind and manner of action. Behavior was strictly divided between masculine and feminine, but both men and women were expected to satisfy their most basic sexual and aggressive instincts in ways that were coded in manners and cloaked in euphemisms so that correct behavior seemed to deny the passions it satisfied. Repression was an essential strategy in subordinating emotion to industry. The secret of successful acting, then, was to suggest the most powerful and basic human instincts without acknowledging that one was doing so.[6]

American acting and playwriting were responding to a subtle shift in the culture's social code that is normally said to have been marked by the plays of Eugene Scribe and Tom Robertson, and which was generally apparent after 1870. Melodramatic writing and acting had emphasized effect. Plays were constructed as a series of scenes, each of which culminated in a fresh revelation of emotional power, each scene being more powerful than the one preceding it. Successful melodrama depended on such a sequence reaching an apparently insoluble impasse in which the triumph of the villain over the virtue of the hero or heroine seemed inevitable. A surprising revelation at the last minute then dissolved the impasse, and the villain was exposed and punished. All of Boucicault's major plays exhibit this pattern.

In pursuit of effect, playwrights suppressed or ignored cause. The coherence of the immediate situation, not to mention that of the whole story, was unimportant so long as the effect was big enough. Such writing obviously encourages an equivalent style of acting, and both are highly reflective. The aim is to stun the audience, not entice it. The acceptability of such conventions was gradually undermined by Newtonian science. Newton's paradigm was predicated on a symmetrical appropriateness between cause and effect, and gradually that assumption penetrated everyday thinking. Just as in life where people learned to look for adequate and appropriate causes for behavior, they came to expect that dramatic and theatrical effects would be justified by appropriate causation. Scribe and Robertson broke with tradition by providing a clear, coherent logic of apparent causation for their effects, and actors in their plays began to do the same. The result was a significant shift away from reflection toward absorption, which was generally described as a shift away from the overtly theatrical. Generally, it was a shift away from effect for its own sake or effect that appeared to acknowledge the presence of the audience.[7]

In Great Britain, the age of the great actor-managers was dying with the century. The retirement of Henry Irving left only Wilson Barrett and Herbert Beerbohm Tree, and Barrett died suddenly and unexpectedly in 1902. What they shared was the view that an actor's job was creative rather than interpretive; roles should be shaped to personality rather than the reverse.[8] The actor as personality became the feature of the performance, and that personality became the basis for creating a coherent, consistent character throughout the play, rather than creating a series of brilliant, startling effects. In short, although the individual star was still the focus of attention, the star's playing moved away from the reflective to the absorptive, inviting the audience to join, to share, in the exploration of a complex personality instead of being astonished and awed by it.

The retirement of Edwin Booth signaled a similar passing of an older generation in the United States. However, the American stage was filled with a rising generation of actors, most of whom were influenced by the coherent, restrained style of their patron saints, Joseph Jefferson and Louisa Lane Drew. Chief among these were her son, John, and her grandchildren, Ethel, Lionel, and John Barrymore. John Drew was for many years the leading man in the company directed by Augustin Daly, which was the home of the newer style, and which stressed youth and vitality in a carefully orchestrated ensemble. Other young actors of note who came from it were Otis Skinner and Tyrone Power. The younger generation of actresses was dominated by Ada Rehan at Daly's, Mary Anderson, Viola Allen, and Julia Marlowe, all of whom were more restrained and genteel than the emotional actresses, such as Fanny Davenport and Clara Morris, of the previous generation.

The women are perhaps more important because America's primary classical export to Australia was the young actress. There were eight of them: Louise Pomeroy (1880–1883), Cora Potter (1890, 1896–1897), Edith Crane (1896 and 1900), Maude Jeffries (1897–1898, 1903–1905), Nance O'Neil (1900–1901, 1905), Janet Waldorf (1901–1902), Minnie Tittell Brune (1905–1909), and Margaret Anglin (1908). Because of their multiple, overlapping visits, any attempt at a chronologically organized discussion would become incoherent. It is more reasonable to discuss them in terms of style and reception.

Their success or failure may well have been related to the development of the bushman as the iconic Australian character. He presented a problem in the context of gender roles. The bushman was not only masculine, he was solitary. There was little room for women in his world, and when there was, it was unclear who she might be. It was, however, perfectly clear that none of the traditional Victorian female gender roles (*Angel of the House*, *Siren*, *Soiled Dove*, *Fallen Woman*) would do. American actresses in the traditional repertory, as well as those in popular frontier and crime melodramas, may have presented certain qualities of strength and independence that eventually contributed to the creation of the Australian bush girl, first clearly defined in *The Squatter's Daughter* (1907).[9]

While contributing to the construction of a national female icon may have been their most significant effect, American actresses also had to satisfy two other complementary sets of expectations. First, there was the expectation that they would act in a style suitable to the elite repertory. Second, there was an expectation that their representation of their gender would conform to the notion of what was socially appropriate for a woman. In their Australian careers, Janet Waldorf, Margaret Anglin, Edith Crane, and Maude Jeffries encompass the late Victorian ideal of womanliness in both ways.

They fit the audience's expectations of a generally quieter, more coherent style that reflected a growing national self-confidence. Federation confirmed the existence of Australia as an independent territory and culture within the British empire, and self-possession was the mark of cultural maturity. Since such a trait had been the hallmark of Jefferson's acting, and since it was the reigning influence on the American stage, it is not surprising that younger American players were increasingly accepted in Australia. Moreover, they were generally acceptable as young ladies on stage. With the exception of Janet Waldorf's reception in Melbourne and Adelaide discussed later, they made their characters socially acceptable. Rosalind, Beatrice, Viola, and Katherine are not passive. They are active, independent agents in shaping their own destinies. However, at the appropriate moment in the story, they yield gracefully to the man they love. That final appearance of submission was essential to keeping the character within the limits of social acceptability as defined by the middle class, which continued to stress piety, purity, submissiveness, and domesticity as the virtues by means of which a woman proved herself more powerful than a man.[10]

Within this first group of actresses, Louise Pomeroy, Janet Waldorf, and Margaret Anglin seem to belong together because each offered novel interpretations that highlighted their independence from tradition. By contrast, Edith Crane and Maude Jeffries continued to retail traditional Victorian attitudes and traditions to an audience that preferred them.

Louise Pomeroy

Representing a younger generation of actors, Louise Pomeroy had begun her career in New York City in the style and repertory of Mary Anderson, Fanny Davenport, and Adelaide Neilson. It was this style that Essie Jenyns had the opportunity to observe as she supported Pomeroy, playing Celia to her Rosalind, Olivia to her Viola, and Ophelia to her Hamlet. Apart from seasons in New Zealand and India, Pomeroy played steadily in Australia from 2 October 1880 until 17 October 1883.

Slightly more than half her performances were of Shakespearean roles. Rosalind, Viola, and Juliet were equally favored, followed closely by Imogen, Cleopatra, and the dual role of Hermione/Perdita. She played Hamlet a dozen times, occasionally offering Lady Macbeth and Beatrice. The rest of her repertory was divided between suffering heroines in *Camille*, *Leah the Forsaken*, *Led Astray*, and *Pique*, and the witty ladies of *London Assurance*, *She Stoops to Conquer*, and *The School for Scandal*.

At first, her acting was described as marred by her American accent, which was "rich and unmistakable" (*Age*, 15 November 1880). It was remarked upon, not because it existed, but because it obtruded, suggesting that Australian audiences had come to tolerate some Americanism of speech:

> If she were to bestow only a small tithe of the attention she pays to the preparation of her impersonations generally to the correction of those Americanisms that occur a little too often, her representations would be marvels of stage art.
>
> (*Age*, 20 December 1880)

The *Advertiser* was more forgiving:

There is a lingering trace of the American intonation...which of itself tells somewhat against her, but as
her voice has a sweet melodious ring...varying from tone
to tone throughout a considerable range, this defect was
not at all painfully noticeable.

(7 February 1881)

A year later the same paper congratulated her for the
degree to which she had overcome it (8 May 1882).

Dr. Neild praised her physical action: "when she moves
she speaks. There is no sound, but all the story is told"
(*Australasian*, 27 November 1880), but it was clear that in
comedy, her physical action exceeded what the critics
regarded as proper for a young lady. The *Argus* noted that
Viola "would never run after Sir Andrew Aguecheek and
prod him in the back with a sword" (6 December 1880), nor
did it think that Rosalind would be "likely to indulge in
such...by-play as getting behind Celia, and spreading out
the latter's skirts so as to conceal her own liberally-
displayed legs when she hears that Orlando is approach-
ing" (18 April 1881). Though these qualities "appeared to
please the audience," they did not please most of the critics.
The *Age* characterized her as "a merry hoyden, who skips
about the stage like a romping schoolgirl" (5 June 1881).

In tragic roles, she succeeded almost unreservedly. She
combined passion with innocent grace and communicated
an illusion of the inner life of the character. Her Juliet was
not "a dreaming poetic girl," but a "woman, with...blood
running like fire in her veins, and intensifying every
passion" (*SMH*, 3 April 1882), while in her Imogen, Dr.
Neild noted that "psychicaly[sic], you discover all that you
desire" (*Australasian*, 4 December 1880).

In other roles, it seems to have been her ability to suggest passion without betraying a regal bearing that

appealed to her audiences. Nowhere was this combination more effective than when she played Hermione. Noting that Leontes's jealousy seemed even less motivated than Othello's, the *Age* critic commended Pomeroy: "She cleverly gave just enough color in her by-play and action when conversing with Polixenes to give a king with a diseased mind cause for suspicion" (22 April 1881). Dr. Neild proclaimed that she had "discovered the true meaning of Cleopatra...all her senses tuned to the highest pitch of capable apprehension; a soul flooded with the glory of an exquisite sensuousness" (*Australasian*, 4 June 1881), yet her passion never disfigured her, said the *Herald* speaking of her "radiant beauty" and "regal grace" (27 February 1882).

Her Hamlet attracted careful attention. She was the only actress to attempt the role in Australia after Louisa Cleveland, and while the critics were unanimous that a woman could never succeed in the part, they gave her credit for the care and intelligence with which she tried. Her first performance of the role was in Ballarat, and the *Australasian*'s correspondent reported that "cheer upon cheer rose from the audience" (5 August 1882). Hers was a modern Hamlet, marked by the use of a blonde wig, lowered vocal pitch, and subdued line readings. Though intelligent and clear, she failed to satisfy the demand for the "abiding gloom of an overmastering grief" that Booth was so successful at portraying (*Argus*, 21 August 1882). For all his reservations, however, Dr. Neild approved of the new style of representation:

> She gives a version of the character which is true, regarded from the psychological stand-point. ...She at once challenges admiration by the vigour, the clearness, and the absolute earnestness of her acting. She gives herself wholly to the character. She forgets, as far as it is possible...that she is a woman, and becomes the prince.
>
> (*Australasian*, 17 July 1883)

Janet Waldorf

Janet Waldorf came to Australia at the beginning of her career, and her reception reflected the audience's perception of appropriate gentility. After three years of private study with Ada Dow Currier (famous for preparing Julia Marlowe for the start of her career in 1887), she had toured the Western states with Norval McGregor for two seasons to increasing success in Marlowe's repertory (*Ingomar*, *The Hunchback*, *Romeo and Juliet*, *As You Like It*, and *Twelfth Night*). According to McGregor, it was Ada Dow's idea to tour the Pacific rim because "she had been over a good part of the route before" (*Dramatic Mirror*, 3 August 1903). From April 1899 to April 1903, they toured the English-speaking settlements of Japan, China, the Philippines, Malaysia, and India, as well as Australia and New Zealand, often playing with local amateurs. After a visit with her parents in Pittsburgh, Waldorf returned to play again in India until she was brought back to the United States in the autumn of 1904 to replace Viola Allen in the national tour of Hall Caine's *The Eternal City*.

Her visits to Australia were opportunistic. In her first, she came from India to Western Australia, playing in Perth and the mining towns around Kalgoorlie between 15 May and 29 June 1901. Later, while playing in New Zealand, she wrote friends that she could not get dates to play in the major Australian cities because the theatres were booked too far in advance, and it was only a pair of disasters that gave her an opportunity.

At great expense, Williamson had brought out an English company to play the American sensation *Ben Hur*, with its large cast and complex treadmills on which the horses ran during the climactic chariot race. Shortly after they opened in Sydney, bubonic plague broke out, and the source of the infection was traced to the hotel adjoining Her Majesty's Theatre where they were playing. The production was forced to close until the infestation subsided, but no sooner had it reopened, the theatre burned to the ground. Williamson was obligated to the actors by contract, but he could not now play Ben Hur because the machinery was ruined. Suddenly he needed a star, or at least a fresh face, to head up this group of actors, so he gambled on Janet Waldorf.

She headed Williamson's Royal Dramatic Company in Sydney, Melbourne, and Adelaide from April through June 1902 in a repertory that included *As You Like It*, *Romeo and Juliet*, and *Twelfth Night*, along with W. G. Wills's *Royal Divorce*. Both her style and reception reminded one of Louise Pomeroy, though she was undoubtedly influenced by the energetic playing of Ada Rehan at Daly's.[11] She was well-liked in Sydney where critics approved of both her acting style and her representation of the feminine. The *Telegraph* thought her Rosalind, "a good performance, marked by dignity, modesty, and simplicity, and was materially aided by the actress' tact in wisely exercising restraint, and in her delightful freedom from mannerisms" (21 April 1902), and repeated its praise for her Juliet: "There is one strikingly commendable feature about everything Miss Waldorf attempts, it is her propriety of action, and demeanor, and without being tame, she tempers her fire with a judicious restraint" (28 April 1902). In his scrapbook, the *Herald* critic, Gerald Marr Thompson, wrote, "Not a star but a good actress."[12]

Otherwise, her comedy was subject to the same criticism as Louise Pomeroy's had been. While the *Argus* approved, "Miss Waldorf has a graceful manner, and plenty of variety in facial expression. When dressed as a boy she was admirably free from the tendency to 'swagger,' and preserved the femininity of the character most successfully" (5 May 1902), the more conservative *Age* did not: "She exaggerates the physical mobility of Rosalind to the extent of making her occasionally hoydenish, and does not take sufficiently into account that she was a Duke's daughter" (5 May 1902). There were similar objections to her Viola and Beatrice. The *Argus* called her duel with Sir Andrew "genuine burlesque" (19 May 1902), and the *Age* described her Beatrice as "a romping schoolgirl" (5 June 1902). The *Bulletin*, in its usually ironic way, touched on at least one factor that made Janet Waldorf both appealing to some and unacceptable to others:

> Janet Waldorf's not unnatural pride in her shapely legs is rather a handicap on *As You Like It*. The fair Yank never lets a chance pass for displaying her beauteous form, and the cloak she wears is held constantly behind her for fear it should interrupt the view. That much is all right, but the contrast of Janet's plump and symmetrical under-standings with the misshaped spindleshanks of the male supers turns the latter into grotesque degenerates.
>
> (24 May 1902:25)

She was too much the high-spirited, egalitarian American girl, unacceptable to many critics in the elite repertory, but popular with large portions of the audience.

Margaret Anglin

The opposite of Janet Waldorf, Margaret Anglin came to Australia for the second half of 1908 as an established star in search of a career change. A product of Charles Frohman's Empire Theatre School in New York City, where pupils were coached by the English actor Nelson Wheat-croft, Anglin had supported such leading men as James O'Neill, E. H. Sothern, and Richard Mansfield before she emerged as a star at the beginning of the century in the title role of *Mrs. Dane's Defense*. From then on, her career was managed by the actor Henry Miller, with whom she starred in her greatest success, William Vaughn Moody's Western drama, *The Great Divide*, from 1906 through 1908. She says she wanted a change of management and repertory, and her biographer suggests that she also wanted to end a romantic relationship with Miller, a relationship she always denied.[13] J. C. Williamson's offer of a six-month tour seemed a good way to accomplish her goals.

Her first three productions were two melodramas that emphasized the comic, *The Thief*, adapted from the French of Henri Bernstein, and *The Truth* by America's most successful commercial playwright, Clyde Fitch. She and her American co-star, Henry Kolker, played them in a quiet natural style that was popular with both press and audiences. All the reviews commented on the ease of her playing: the Melbourne critic of *The Bulletin* thought that "Of the few great actresses Australia has seen during the past 25 years...Miss Anglin is perhaps the most simply natural" (27 August 1908), while *The Age* observed, "So natural is she, so entirely free from all artificialities of stagecraft, that one runs almost the risk of suspecting her veracity even as a private citizen" (14 September 1908). Her single failure was in a few performances of *Camille* in Melbourne. The play was too creaky, and she was too robust, to persuade an audience that she was dying at all, much less of consumption.

She said that she had intended to try Shakespeare from the outset, and that Williamson opposed her on commercial grounds. She seems to have talked him around, and her *Taming of the Shrew* proved so popular that he asked for another and got *Twelfth Night*. Her Katherine may have been based on that of Ada Rehan, the reigning shrew of the American stage, but critics found it too quiet and lady-like: "Miss Anglin makes it abundantly clear...that behind the vixenish shrew there is a noble, imperious gentlewoman. ...Miss Anglin never for a moment takes the shrewish scenes in an ugly spirit of violent ill-temper" (*Argus*, 28 September 1908). However, a contributor to the *Bulletin*'s Poverty Point objected that she "screams, chokes, gurgles in her frenzy" (26 November 1908), which another correspondent attributed to the reviews which had persuaded her that the Australian audience wanted Shakespeare "chuck't at 'em" (3 December 1908). Whatever the case, by the time she played Katherine in Adelaide and Sydney, all the reviews agreed that she managed a perfect transition from the violent to the docile in the course of the action:

> In the opening scenes her voice was shrill yet raucous, and there was a passionate irascibility in all her words, acts, and gestures. ...Then in the last act...she comes trippingly at her husband's bidding, and with charming grace and mellow voice recites the speech.
>
> (*Advertiser*, 9 November 1908)

By contrast her Viola was found properly romantic. While characterized as "coy," she avoided the burlesque elements that Australian critics objected to in Pomeroy's and Waldorf's performances a decade earlier.

As popular and polished as she was, Anglin was more strongly supported than many actresses in Australia. Her co-star, Henry Kolker, was a product of the German language theatre in Milwaukee, and while the critics found him stiff, they also found him powerful. He was, perhaps, a bit too savage as Petruchio (*Bulletin*, 26 November 1908), but ideal as Orsino. She also had the services of George Titheradge, a fine, popular actor of long standing in Australia, who played a "very high and very dry" Malvolio (*SMH*, 7 December 1908).

As well as pleasing Australian audiences with her quieter, more natural acting, Margaret Anglin succeeded for a time in shifting from contemporary drama to classic. After returning to the United States, she produced *Antigone* and

Electra in both California and New York City, and during 1913–1914, toured *Taming of the Shrew* and *Twelfth Night*, but after the World War, she returned to the popular melodrama of the besieged and threatened woman, roles which she redeemed by the intelligence and humor of her playing.

Edith Crane

Edith Crane is the first of two successful American actresses who specialized in historical romance, which was accepted as part of the elite repertory of the time. Undoubtedly, its respectability had been secured by the popularity of the historical novels of Walter Scott, Charles Dickens, Bulwer Lytton, and others, but in the main, they appealed because they translated the muscular Christianity of Tom Brown's *Schooldays* into the widely accepted conventions of melodrama as an antidote to Imperial corruption and exhaustion. Her real triumph, however, was to convert a socially marginal character into an idealized stage persona: the angel of the house, the still center from which the man drew energy and motivation and to whom he returned for healing and forgiveness.

Edith Crane was a luminous center. Trained for three years (1890–1893) in small roles at Augustin Daly's theatre, she soon found her great role, Trilby, the title role of Paul Potter's dramatization of George Du Maurier's novel. A. M. Palmer chose her to replace Virginia Harned, who had created the role, and J. C. Williamson brought her and several other actors from that company to tour all the cities except Perth between April and July of 1896.

She became so identified with Trilby that the role's qualities defined her acting. Trilby is a young girl of a lower class, who makes her living in Paris by posing nude for artists. In the novel, Du Maurier makes it clear that she is also sexually free and naive: "No pressure of want, no temptation of greed or vanity, had ever been factors in urging Trilby on her downward path," and while this element was excised from the stage version, contemporary criticism assumed that most of the audience had read the book.[14] Even if they had not, Trilby's appearance, bare-footed, would have provided a suggestive sign. The point, of course, is that Trilby is utterly unsuitable as a wife for the well-born English painter William Bagot (Little Billee) who loves her. At his family's request, she leaves Paris. Her sacrifice, along with her suffering and death at the hands of the musician-hypnotist, Svengali, permits the audience to weep for her without betraying its standards of public sexual morality.

In her playing, Crane seems to have suggested that, in spite of appearances, Trilby is a lady. The *Sydney Telegraph* notice is quite clear about that: "Miss Crane…is a tall, beautiful actress. …She does not suggest the Trilby who had passed quite a lot of time in the gutter, but a…creature full of warm life…ladylike in her manner" (18 May 1896), and the reviews from Adelaide, Brisbane, and Hobart all confirm this description. Even her vocal quality, described as "metallic" (*Bulletin*, 14 September 1901) was thought to be an advantage since it suggested Trilby's tone-deafness, so central to the story. Similarly, Reuben Fax's Svengali was praised for not being "all fantastic tricks" as Beerbohm Tree played the role in England (*Telegraph*, 16 May 1896).

When Williamson brought her back to Australia and New Zealand in 1900, she was accompanied by her husband, Tyrone Power, as her co-star. The grandson of the Irish comic actor, this Tyrone Power had been sent to Florida as a young man to learn the orange-growing business, but he ran away and went on the stage in early 1886. By the fall of 1891, he had found his way to Daly's where he supported John Drew and, incidentally, met Edith

Crane. They married in 1898 when he left Daly for good, and they attempted to become a starring couple.

Trilby was still the play they performed most often, and his Svengali seemed as much a gentleman as her Trilby was a lady. Their other successes (each played about half as often as Trilby) were Hall Caine's *The Christian*, John Martin-Harvey's *The Only Way* (based on Dickens's *A Tale of Two Cities*), and a version of *Tess of the d'Urbervilles*.

The notice of *Trilby* in the *West Australian* suggests the restraint and propriety with which they played what in other hands would have been crudest melodrama:

> In the lighter scenes she was free and graceful. ...Miss Crane showed herself capable of rising to those danger-ous higher flights which test the capacity of an actor to the utmost. ...Miss Crane is a wise actress in that she knows when to stop. ...Mr. Tyrone Power...did not exag-gerate. ...Mr. Power had the good sense and good taste, not always sufficiently manifest on the Australian stage to exercise artistic restraint.
>
> (18 April 1900)

In all cases, Crane was found to be the apotheosis of "womanly tenderness and fascination" (*West Australian*, 23 April 1900).

Other reviewers made the same point about Power's Svengali: "The demoniacal aspect...was somewhat sup-pressed, and the character was made less repulsive than the ideal Svengali" (*Age*, 3 September 1900); "forcible...less nervous and spider-like than Mr. Fax" (*Argus*, 3 September 1900). Such restraint was especially important for Power, since his other parts, Alec D'Urberville and Sydney Carton, were not socially acceptable, the one an aristocratic brute, the other a drunk. Yet, repeatedly, the reviews praise Power's manliness and subtlety. Only the *Advertiser* expressed gentle dissent to his playing of Carton: "Mr.

Power somewhat accentuated the grosser attributes of the young barrister, without giving to them the tempering grace of refinement" (27 June 1900).

They had been so successful that when their contract with Williamson expired, they presented themselves under their own management in Melbourne. In seven weeks, they were bankrupt with debts of $8,000 and assets of $1,250. Sadly, theatrical virtue did not translate into commercial success. They returned to the United States where her career was ended by cancer, but he continued to play successfully on stage and in film for many years.

Maude Jeffries

Unquestionably, however, it was Maude Jeffries who became the most successful American representative of the ideal woman in Australian theatre. Apart from a single production in 1888, her preparation for stardom was a single season at Daly's in 1890. The English actor-manager Wilson Barrett hired her as his leading lady, and with him, she made one tour of Australia in 1898. After his death, she acted with Tree and returned with Julius Knight at the head of Williamson's dramatic company. She remained in Australia, marrying in 1904 and retiring halfway through 1906.[15]

Barrett's repertory featured his own dramatizations of successful novels, *The Sign of the Cross* and *Claudian* (stories of Christian sacrifice in Rome) and *The Manxman* (a gritty tale of sexual betrayal and punishment). With him, she also appeared as the faithful wife, Nellie Denver, in *The Silver King*, and as Ophelia and Desdemona. The Knight–Jeffries repertory featured such costume dramas as Clyde Fitch's *Monsieur Beaucaire*, Barrett's *The Way of the Cross*, Hall Caine's *The Eternal City*, David Belasco's *Darling of the Gods*, and W. G. Wills's *A Royal Divorce*, as well as some melodramatic realism in *The Silver King* and Tolstoy's *Resurrection*. In every case, Maude Jeffries played a character who behaved as popular morality said a woman should in such situations. She was the constant martyr, either to her husband's or lover's needs, or in remorse for her own sins.

Part of her unvarying success in Australia was that, because of her training under Barrett, she appeared "essentially English" (*Advertiser*, 15 April 1906). That meant that in all roles, she was seen as appropriately forceful in her emotions without violating the limits of restraint that decorum insisted was a woman's true nature: "Maud Jeffries adopted restrained methods as Nellie Denver, whose grief was delineated as inward and silent" (*Advertiser*, 24 July 1905). Necessarily, this produced a highly absorptive style. As Josephine in *A Royal Divorce*, she "seemed so much in earnest that one sometimes finds it difficult to dissociate her from the part she delineates with such wonderful realism" (*Courier*, 14 July 1904). Her behavior outside the theatre was also modest. She went to no parties and gave no interviews.

However, she was not sexless. Everyone commented on her physical beauty, and the *Argus* described her performance in *The Manxsman* as "aglow with vitality—willful, passionate, seductive" (10 January 1890). Nor did she always play an aristocrat. In *Resurrection*, the *Age* marveled at her "quick changes…from drunken recklessness to unavailing regret, from desperate resentment…to broken sobs…from hatred to gratitude, from resignation to hopelessness" (14 September 1903), but as the *Argus* noted: "Treated with less adriotness and tact the character of Katusha might have been made simply appalling. But Miss Jeffries throughout always permits some little glimpse of the woman to be seen" (14 September 1903).

Unquestionably, however, the role with which she became most closely identified was Mercia in *The Sign of the*

Cross. Curiously, Barrett did not include it in his repertory when they visited Australia, but she and Knight more than compensated. The *Argus* thought her "The embodiment of sweetness and light, beautiful as an angel in voice and pose, with face and form hewn from the virgin marble of old Pentelicus" (9 May 1904) and all other reviews agreed. As her photographs make clear, she was the personification of Pre-Raphaelite purity and sensuality.

There were also three men from the United States who presented the classical repertory, all of them contemporaries of Louise Pomeroy. W. H. Leake was a successful player in the American idiom of the gold rush melodrama. Subsequently, however, he failed in leading Shakespearean roles, and found only limited acceptance as a supporting player in the classic repertory. Schooled in the style of Forrest whom he supported in Philadelphia and New York, he had toured with Pomeroy in the United States. In Australia, he appeared with her again, as well as with George Crichton Miln and William E. Sheridan, who succeeded in meeting the Australian audience's taste for a style of Shakespearean performance that embodied the values of the rising middle class.

George Crichton Miln

English by birth and public schooling, Miln had been a minister and had written and lectured on Shakespeare. He took to the stage in Chicago in 1882 and began playing in Australia on 6 October 1886. Apart from a month in New Zealand, he continued until 28 October 1890, after which he went on to the theatres of Asia and India.

Miln's repertory favored Richard III, Hamlet, Othello, Marc Antony, and Antony (in that order), but including Romeo, Shylock, and Macbeth. A small handful of older costume plays filled out his roles (*Richelieu, The Fool's*

Revenge, Damon and Pythias, and *Ingomar*), but nearly 85 percent of his performances in Australia were in Shakespearean roles—more than any American except W. E. Sheridan.

Miln was earnest and respectable. Because of his previous professions, he was always treated respectfully as a producer, even when reviewers disliked his work as an actor; and he received considerable public sympathy and support after his bankruptcy at the end of his Melbourne season in December 1889. As Eric Irvin observed, "Wherever he went he quickly made useful friends among the several grades of society."[16]

Miln was a ranter whose powerful, pleasant voice and correct enunciation overcame the excessive violence of his physical action. As the *Brisbane Courier* summarized the style:

> Mr. Miln...belongs to the Kemble school of actors. His...style may be characterised as that of robust classicism as contrasted with that of Irving. Mr. Miln's rich, deep musical voice, which he modulates with much artistic effect, is especially adapted for the classic... style. ...His presence is dignified, and...free from obtrusive mannerisms.
>
> (19 November 1888)

The effect of his speaking is also apparent in *The Age*'s description of his playing in Julius Caesar:

> The lament, when Antony is left...alone with the corpse, was spoken with such force and fire as to electrify the audience, who made the theatre ring again and again with applause. The funeral oration was also a masterpiece of acting.
>
> (8 April 1889)

Whatever the merits of his pulpit-trained voice, his stage action was altogether too violent for Australian taste. In Sydney, the *Daily Telegraph* thought his Hamlet too graphically mad, and noted that his Richard III "was disfigured by the worst extravagancies of an old-fashioned school," the climactic duel lasting for fully ten minutes (22 October 1888). *The Age* agreed that his Hamlet was too vigorous, while the *Advertiser* thought his Shylock "a remarkably robust old savage" (21 October 1890).

Although an old-fashioned actor like Leake, he was a modern producer, following the examples of Samuel Phelps and Charles Kean, who understood the appeal of lavish, historically accurate spectacle to the middle class, appropriating aristocratic history to support their accession to power. It was the cost of the scenery and the extra actors that bankrupted him, not a lack of audience. Australians supported remarkable runs of consecutive performances in Melbourne: *Richard III* and *Julius Caesar* (eighteen each), *Othello* (nineteen, with Miln switching to Iago halfway through), *Hamlet* and *Antony and Cleopatra* (twenty-four each).

William E. Sheridan

One of the most popular American actors of Shakespeare in Australia, William E. Sheridan visited twice. The first visit lasted more than a year (22 July 1882 to 8 September 1883), but the second was cut short. He opened in Sydney on 20 November 1886, but was ill and stopped playing after 22 December. He suffered a stroke on 12 May and died on the fifteenth. As evidence of his popular and professional standing, a monument to mark his grave in Sydney's Waverley Cemetery was erected by public subscription.

Sheridan was the most reputable American actor to play in Australia during the period. After an apprenticeship in the provinces and service in the Union army, he played seconds to Edwin Booth in New York City, and became a leading man in Philadelphia. As a touring star after 1881, he was one of a group of tragedians (including Thomas Keene, Louis James, and Charles Hanford) who supplied most of America's provincial audience with performances in a style shaped by both Edwin Forrest and Edwin Booth. In this style, the actor contrived to represent tumultuous passion and effect rapid transition without violating the audience's sense of appropriateness, suggesting emotional extremity without vocal or physical excess. Sheridan was never criticized for exaggeration the way Leake and Miln had been. Surviving descriptions suggest that it was by a combination of correct verse reading and understatement, emphasized with facial expression and pantomimic stage action, that he was able to achieve the effect.

More than half his Shakespearean performances were as Lear, but he would also play Richard III, Othello, Hamlet, and Shylock. The rest of his repertory was made up of Sir Giles Overreach (in *A New Way to Pay Old Debts*) and the leading roles in *Louis XI*, *The Marble Heart*, and *The Corsican Brothers*. His Australian reputation was based on *Lear* and *Louis XI*.

His beginning in Sydney was unpromising. Not only was he forced to appear at the Queen's Theatre, "in which it was considered the legitimate drama could hardly find an abiding place," but he "came amongst us...with a reputation purely American, and but very few...were disposed to admit his claims to a position...similar to that held by Brooke, Kean, Barry, Sullivan, Creswick" (*Daily Telegraph*, 7 August 1882). Moreover, the writer thought Sheridan showed "remarkable daring" in beginning with *Lear*, and was pleased to report that:

Mr. Sheridan possesses a powerful well-modulated voice, and most wonderful facial expression; but he is without any of those mannerisms, either in speech or action, that are usually considered inseparable from actors who have passed any length of time in America.

(*Daily Telegraph*, 24 July 1882)

The *Sydney Morning Herald* praised his taste:

While avoiding the thundering style of denunciation and rapidity of speech which many actors who claim eminence have chosen mistakenly to adopt, he was on all occasions powerful and never failed to impress upon his audience an appropriate emphasis of Shakespeare's admirable language.

(24 July 1882)

His Lear was equally praised in Melbourne:

It is not always so much in the words that Mr. Sheridan exhibits his power as in some of the pauses. Thus when he first becomes alive to Regan's ingratitude, the silence and the look...are more powerfully descriptive than words.

(*Age*, 4 September 1882)

The *Australasian* agreed, "When he reaches the mad stage, he is abundant in expressive manifestation, and his tenderness over the body of Cordelia is unquestionably full of poetic beauty" (9 September 1882). Thirty years later, the habitués of the Bulletin's "Poverty Point" accepted the claim that his was the best among the few Lears Australians had seen (14 May 1911).

As Louis XI his death scene was praised for its reality and technical skill, "the sinkings and exhaustions of the king being rendered with an almost ghastly fidelity...and the slightest whisper of the great actor was distinctly audible" (*Daily Telegraph*, 14 December 1882), and when he offered Hamlet, even though not perfect in his lines, "Many present who had seen both Creswick and Irving compared his impersonation favourably with that of the former, and almost on a par with that of the latter actor" (*Daily Telegraph*, 17 March 1883).

American players of Shakespeare contributed to both the quantity and quality of Shakespearean performance in Australia during the 1880s. They accounted for slightly less than one-third of the total number of performances in the cities, they reintroduced some plays into the repertory, and the successful ones offered a stylistic alternative to the English tradition. Leake failed because, whatever his talent, his vocal and physical representations were too violent for emerging middle-class taste. Miln, too, was physically excessive, but his powerful, well-modulated pulpit voice overcame that defect because the audience valued the words over the actions. Sheridan and Pomeroy presented the American version of a new, quieter style that appealed to a middle-class audience which celebrated its growing cultural influence by defining its parlor as the seat of power. Moreover, in Pomeroy's influence on Essie Jenyns, this contribution continued. Thus, American players and styles contributed to the cultural agenda of an emerging nation. England provided the dominant tone for Australian culture, but American players of Shakespeare provided a tonic to the sound.

CHAPTER 9

The Elite Repertory After 1880, Part Two: Challenging Expectations

THREE OTHER AMERICAN ACTRESSES SUCCEEDED with the Australians, overlapping Janet Waldorf, Margaret Anglin, Edith Crane, and Maud Jeffries. This second group, however, challenged expectations rather than meeting them. These actresses demanded that the audience meet them on their own terms, and they were generally successful in that demand. One might suggest that while the first group represented the received ideal of womanliness, this second group represented the emerging demand by women for a new identity.

Cora Potter

As the Victorian Siren, Cora Potter challenged her audiences onstage and off. Married at eighteen to James Brown, she was slender, red-haired, violet-eyed, beautiful, spoiled, and bored. Public recitations and amateur theatricals for charity provided an outlet, beginning in 1881. In 1886, she left her husband and daughter for London and the stage: "I knew my husband did not care for me. We had been a disappointment to each other from the first."[1]

Her professional debut was as Annie Sylvester in Wilkie Collins's *Man and Wife* at London's Haymarket Theatre, 29 March 1887, with the Prince of Wales in the audience. Her reviews were unanimously unfavorable, but Collins encouraged her, and in October, she repeated the role in New York City. In between, she had played the title role in *Mademoiselle Bressier* at London's Gaiety Theatre, where her leading man was Kyrle Bellew, who accompanied her to New York. Arriving in Australia as a merchant seaman, Bellew had turned to journalism before going on the stage there in 1875. Subsequently, he made a career as a romantic leading man in both Great Britain and the United States. He served Potter in that capacity, as well as being her stage manager and her lover.[2]

For the next three years, they toured the United States. In an autobiography that is primarily an account of her social triumphs, Cora Potter nevertheless refers to her first Australian tour as "that wonderful event in my life."[3] She opened as Camille at Melbourne's Princess's Theatre on 1 March 1890. She closed in mid-December after also playing Sydney and Adelaide. Between then and her return (6 June 1896), she and Bellew toured Great Britain, the United States, and twice played the Asia-Pacific rim from South Africa to Japan. After a year in Australia and New Zealand, she settled in London, where she continued to appear in plays, recitals, and the music halls until her retirement to the south of France.

Cora Potter delighted in attention and was not averse to genteel scandal. As an amateur, she had recited a poem ("*Ostler Joe*" by G. R. Sims) for a charity event. The verse narrative of a country girl who is seduced, becomes an actress and prostitute, and is eventually forgiven by her faithful husband, was so shocking that the sister of President Grover Cleveland left the room. The incident was reported in the newspapers, and she recounts the event in her autobiography with pleasure at the notoriety.[4] Her relationship with Kyrle Bellew was always tinged with scarlet because she was not divorced by Potter until 1902, and both her repertory and her style of playing seemed deliberately provocative. She was a vivid, energetic personality, just what an American was expected to be.

Her American reputation was largely created by her portrayal of Shakespeare's Cleopatra, in a text arranged by Bellew. She emphasized Cleopatra's sensuality. Her costumes were transparent, so that the shape of her legs and bosom, clad in flesh-colored tights, was always visible, and her sinuous embraces of Marc Antony left little to the audience's imagination. All the New York critics were horrified by both the text and the performance except Nym Crinkle, who praised Bellew and Potter for giving Shakespearean performance its true spirit, rather than reducing it to the propriety of the Victorian drawing room. Nevertheless, he made it clear that her performance was distinctly modern, noting that her Cleopatra was a type of woman that could be seen any afternoon strolling along Fifth Avenue.[5]

Her repertory featured a small gallery of passionate women. She appeared most often in Sardou's *La Tosca*, followed by *Camille*. During her first visit to Australia, she played Juliet nearly as often as she played Tosca, and she played Hero in Bellew's *Hero and Leander* about half as often. For her second visit, she added Rosalind and Portia to her Shakespearean repertory. She also offered Santuzza in Giovanni Verga's *Cavaleria Rusticana*, and Violet Gresham in Tom Taylor's *David Garrick*. In addition, she regularly played Kate Hardcastle, Lady Teazle, and Pauline Deschapelles, though only about half as often as the tragic roles.

The Australian comic opera star Nellie Stewart called Potter's style sinister: "She clothed her lithe body in such a way as gave an effect of snakiness. Long before the cinema, she was the first of the vampires."[6] If she had any model, it might have been Sara Bernhardt (who played Australia from May to August 1891), but she seems to have played all her parts in the same way, utilizing the same set of personal mannerisms in all of them.[7]

Consequently, her reviews tend to be highly repetitive. Everyone agreed that she was strikingly delicate and beautiful, that her voice was in the low alto range with a harsh edge to it, that she moved and gestured often and with a carefully studied effect. She was praised for certain scenes of greatest intensity, such as the balcony and tomb scenes in *Romeo and Juliet* and the killing of Scarpia in *La Tosca*, and she was criticized for indifference and inaudability in many others. She was quite clearly an extremely reflective actor with a single persona that varied little, if at all.

One either liked her or did not. James Smith was presumably as sympathetic as he could be when reviewing her debut as Camille, remarking on her physical suitability for the role, describing her originality, which he termed as "contradictions" (1 March 1890). He lost patience, however, with her Juliet:

> Her interpretation...appears to be that of a somewhat kittenish young girl...who, being physically and mentally precocious, has often taken part in private theatricals in the family mansion, and has thus acquired a habit of lifting her right arm vertically and extending it horizontally, by way of accompaniment to her conversation; of making little dashes across the stage, head forward, at full speed; of speaking artificially, with a rising and falling inflection of the voice, and a strong emphasis upon a comparatively unimportant word; and of dropping down into an almost sepulchral tone where strong and serious emotion has to be expressed.
>
> (*Argus*, 7 July 1890)

The *Bulletin* writers agreed:

Her attitudes were artificial and labored and affected; her painted visage, with a great mass of black at the outer corner of each eye and a splash of red at the inner one, was an extra-ordinary piece of Impressionist art. ...She rolled her eyes painfully, and made fearful and wonderful mouths, and had strange adventures with her hair; and her Tosca was an artificial creature who couldn't have lived, because she would have wriggled herself to death at an early age.

(22 August 1896)

Yet as absolute as these judgments seem, there were critics who approved and audiences who came in droves. Dr. Neild, obviously contrasting her Camille with his memory of Mary Provost's thirty years before, described her as:

Graceful, lissome, and easy in her movements. ...There are no facial twitchings, no tragic corrugations, no clenchings of the teeth, no rigid fixings of the lower jaw. ...The evidence of large intelligence and strong...feeling is abundant.

(*Australasian*, 8 March 1890)

Acknowledging her tendency to move about too much, he still found her Juliet "eminently girlish. ...It is a strong Juliet" (12 July 1890), and the *Age* agreed: "She depicts Juliet as a child of nature, a true daughter of sunny Italy; full of impulse, passion and fire" (5 July 1890). Neild even liked her in Bellew's *Hero and Leander*, a performance notable for the undress of both stars: "Mrs. Potter's performance...was marked by a consistent sincerity of manner and sobriety of demeanour, which were pleasing" (*Australasian*, 30 August 1890). Indeed Neild's public disagreements with Smith about her became an issue, because as chief critic for the

Argus, which published the *Australasian*, Smith was his boss. Neild resigned rather than shape his opinion to that of his superior. Thus ended the career of Australia's most interesting drama critic whose own eccentric independence matched that of the actress he championed.

Nance O'Neil

Gertrude Lamson wanted to follow her older sister into the theatre. When she applied to manager McKee Rankin of San Francisco's Alcazar Theatre, he cast her as a nun and a prostitute, and from then (16 October 1893) until 1909 managed her life, changed her name, and made her a star. Rankin was a character who would not have been out of place in a story by Mark Twain or Bret Harte. At the beginning of his career, he was handsome, gifted, and successful. Now he was fat, shifty, and broke.[8]

During a ten-year apprenticeship, he had become leading man of A. M. Palmer's company at New York's Union Square Theatre between 1872 and 1875, when it was widely regarded as the artistic equal of the companies of Lester Wallack and Augustin Daly. Like all leading men, he wanted to be a star on his own, which required a vehicle. Attracted to the dramatic possibilities of Joaquin Miller's story, *The First Family of the Sierras*, he added situations, made a scenario, and got another actor to write the dialogue. Then he paid Miller for the rights and opened *The Danites* in Brooklyn on 22 August 1877. He was still playing it when he met Nance O'Neil. For four years, they trouped from city to city, establishing her as a rising star during a season at the Murray Hill Theatre in New York City at the close of 1897. The *Dramatic Mirror* thought that

> Nance O'Neil has no tricking or false effects in her work—there was even less ranting and railing than is

usual—and her acting was of a brilliant and fiery intensity that reminded on forcibly of Clara Morris in her younger days.

(11 December)

During the next three years, she became immensely popular on the Pacific Coast in her repertory of suffering heroines: Leah in *The Jewess* (*Leah the Forsaken*), Nancy Sykes, Magda in Sudermann's play of the same name, Queen Elizabeth in Giacometti's drama, and Camille. Magda, Elizabeth, and Camille were most popular during her tour of Australia between March 1900 and August 1901. However, her visit was also an opportunity to experiment with new plays and characters. Tosca and Fedora were familiar to local audiences, and they proved nearly as popular as Camille. She also added Hedda Gabler, Lady Inger of Ostrat, and Macbeth. Apart from a single performance of Hedda Gabler by Janet Achurch in Brisbane a decade before, the Ibsen plays were new to Australia.

She was the opposite of Cora Potter: powerful rather than petite; assertive rather than seductive. Tall, with a harsh baritone voice that ranged from a hoarse whisper to a banshee shriek, she seemed like a force of nature. Her volcanic surges of emotion were extreme, and spectators were either thrilled or offended. Her acting didn't fit anyone's idea of culture or manners. The *Sydney Telegraph*'s review of her Magda captures a tone repeated in almost every Australian notice:

> She strides the stage almost mannishly, and…creeps close to her victim with pantherish viciousness. …To see her standing with her back to the audience (a favorite attitude with her) and her arms outspread like some dominating queen…is remarkable. …In all her moods, however, the lady is hard, sometimes harsh, and acerbity pervades the whole representation.
>
> (12 March 1900)

Perhaps her most interesting Sydney notice was the opinion that the *Herald*'s reviewer Gerald Marr Thompson recorded in his scrapbook, "In spite of some crudity…in voice and expression, Miss O'Neil is more nearly a great artist than any unknown actress I have ever heard." After witnessing Act 3 of *Magda* again, he sat up talking with O'Neil and Rankin, "Miss O'Neil's analysis of Magda full of interest."[9] Thompson and other critics were even pleased with her playing of Hedda Gabler though they detested the play.[10]

Her Lady Macbeth drew conflicting opinions; her strengths seemed to some to be weaknesses. Thompson was her strongest advocate, approving of such unconventional stage business as reading Macbeth's letter while seated, and praising her sleepwalking scene in which her "vacant stare betrayed the mental desolation, and the burthen of the broken heart found voice in accents of poignant anguish" (*SMH*, 9 November 1900). He also noted that she was rewarded with "a tempest of prolonged applause." The *Age* thought, "Her…Lady Macbeth, though strong and impressive, is marked by a tendency to exaggerate the vixenish and ferocious instincts of the woman"; the critic wanted more "intellect," "subtlety," "charm" (6 May 1901). The *Bulletin*, which never liked her, later remembered her performance this way:

> Miss O'Neil took Lady Macbeth in a rush and top-noted from the start. Her stage partner…endeavored to yell up to her, with the result that his voice went to rags. …He complained bitterly…that Nance's embrace-method was to fling herself headlong on top of her stage-lover and weigh him nearly to the floor. …One night…a gallery-boy…yelled. …"Dodge her, little feller!"
>
> (5 April 1906)

Within her own repertory, she could successfully challenge expectation, but any such attempt with Shakespeare was controversial.

From Australia, Rankin, O'Neil, and their company sailed away to Africa where she played in Cape Town and elsewhere before proceeding to Cairo and Alexandria for short seasons. Their goal, however, was London. They offered *Magda*, *Camille*, and *Elizabeth* at the Adelphi Theatre during September 1902.[11] Unfortunately, Bernhardt, Duse, and Mrs. Patrick Campbell had played those roles in recent memory, and the comparisons, while fair, were unflattering. Rankin filed for bankruptcy in October 1904. Among his liabilities was $13,500 in back salary and loans owed to her (*DM*, 24 October 1904). In January, the *Dramatic Mirror* had reported an offer from J. C. Williamson for a second Australian tour. It was a short visit, a single season each in Melbourne, Brisbane, and Sydney between 17 June and 28 September 1905, but they were warmly received. As the *Herald* had written after her failure in London, "Our playgoers admired her, not because of her faults, but in spite of them" (11 October 1902). Magda and Elizabeth remained central to her repertory, but just as often on this visit she played Giacometti's Marie Antoinette and Trilby. The former role was brand new, while she had last played DuMaurier's heroine in 1898. Her success as Trilby was particularly striking in view of Edith Crane's popularity in the role.

All her Australian reviewers agreed that while she had lost none of her power, she played with greater subtlety and femininity. As Magda, the *Age* thought, "She has softened…her exuberant vitality" (19 June), while as Elizabeth, "The imperial rages which form the centerpieces of each act were taken as powerfully as ever, with perhaps a more feminine touch" (3 July). In describing her Trilby, the *Courier Mail* said, "There was a gleaming womanhood defiled not in wantonness, but by the effect of environment" (14 August). Even Magda seemed softer, "Miss O'Neil…was an admirable judge of values, who did not consider it necessary to shriek her passion. She attained the heights…without any ranting or display of undue energy, and…was always convincing" (*Telegraph*, 4 September).

She returned to the United States, continuing to play strong women, such as the mother in Sydney Howard's *The Silver Cord* (1928). One of her last appearances was in Edgar Wallace's *A Criminal At Large*, which was an experimental television broadcast at the New York World's Fair in November 1939.

Minnie Tittell Brune

Of all the American actresses, only Mary Provost matched Tittell Brune's versatility, and only Maggie Moore exceeded her popularity. Her stay in Australia was the longest of any American player, her repertory cut across conventional categories, and she sustained her popularity during the visits of Maude Jeffries, Nance O'Neil, and Margaret Anglin.

One could not have predicted such a result. She had followed her half-sisters, Charlotte and Essie (Esther) onto the California stage in 1887. Between 1889 and 1895, they were leading actresses in Pacific Northwest stock companies, and then she married Clarence M. Brune, a stage-struck lawyer, in Moscow, Idaho, and retired.[12]

In the autumn of 1899, the Brunes returned to the theatre. For two seasons she was a successful leading lady to an established star, first with Frederick Warde, then with Melbourne MacDowell. Clarence assumed supporting roles as both actor and manager of the companies. Finally, for the seasons of 1901 and 1902, Minnie Tittell Brune starred in *Unorna* by Espy Williams, a play she had commissioned, but both seasons were cut short, one by finances, the other by illness. While she had climbed up the theatrical ladder from leading stock actress to star, she stumbled over the last rung.[13]

In the autumn of 1902, Clarence had played a leading role in Theodore Kramer's melodrama, *The Fatal Wedding*, at London's Princess's Theatre, and she seems to have joined him at the end of that season. While he engaged in theatre management, she studied singing and at some point agreed to an engagement as leading lady for one of J. C. Williamson's two dramatic companies.

Her arrival was nearly disastrous. In June 1904, she and Clarence had to be rescued from the P&O liner *Australia*, when it crashed on the rocks outside Port Melbourne, but she reported to rehearsal on time the next day. Clarence proceeded to Sydney where, the next month, he began acting in *His Majesty the King* with Earnest Knight, who had recently acted in that play with Maude Williamson. The reviews were mixed at best, and Ms. Williamson obtained an injunction against the production on the grounds that she owned the rights to it in Australia. Brune returned to the United States in January 1905. By contrast, Minnie's reviews were generally excellent, and, except for well-earned vacations, she acted steadily from August 1904 through June 1909.

Her Australian career can be divided into three phases. From August 1904 through August 1907, her repertory was made up almost entirely of emotional dramas, some standard, some new, several associated with Sarah Bernhardt: Paul Kester's *Dorothy Vernon of Haddon Hall*, Rostand's *L'Aiglon*, *Leah*, *Romeo and Juliet*, *Parsifal*, *Camille*, *Theodora*, *Tosca*, *The Second Mrs. Tanqueray* and *The Light that Failed*, in that order of frequency. In addition, she played one piece in the American idiom, *Sunday*, and one modern comedy-romance, Isreal Zangwil's *Merely Mary Ann*. The former was played the most often of anything in her repertory, while the latter was played more often than *Romeo and Juliet*. From April through August of 1908, she starred in Barrie's *Peter Pan*, after which she played only five pieces: David Belasco's *The Girl of the Golden West*, Cicely Hamilton's comedy-romance, *Diana of Dobson's*, *Sunday*, *Dorothy Vernon*, and *Romeo and Juliet*. In all, she played fifteen roles in Australia, only two of which she had done before. However, only three or four plays accounted for about half the performances in any engagement. Thomas Raceward's *Sunday* was the only piece that she played during the entire five years, and Belasco's play accounted for two-thirds of the performances in her final eight months.

She seemed to be an absorptive actress, whose primary persona was the rebel, who could easily become the larrikin. Her characters rebel against or challenge established social orders and codes of conduct. Juliet and Dorothy Haddon rebel against family loyalty; Sunday, Minnie, and Diana rebel against class and gender distinctions; the Duke of Reichstadt rebels against established political order; and Peter Pan rebels against nature by refusing to become an adult.

Small, slender, with a clear alto voice, she was most popular in roles which stressed her boyish energy: Sunday, the Duke of Reichstadt, Peter Pan, and Juliet. The *Argus* thought that as Sunday, "Miss Brune succeeds more completely as the ingenue little American of the rough mining camp than in any other character in her diversified repertoire for the reason that it is nearer her own individuality" (6 May 1907). The *Sydney Telegraph* commented on her "whole-souled enthusiasm, her easy, natural, unaffected manner" (19 September 1904), while the *Bulletin* astutely noted her mannerisms: "A lot of valuable light artillery in the shape of smiles, pouts, bird-like tiltings of the head, cooings and gigglings. ...Her voice has many tones and semi-tones, and is of unusual clearness" (22 September 1904). It was enthusiastic over her Duke of Reichstadt:

> Her slight, boyish figure and contralto-speaking voice are two magnificent assets...and the artistic, free use she makes of her hands and arms, must be a revelation. ...More breathless attention or greater applause has never been vouchsafed.
>
> (13 October 1904)

The *Age* agreed:

> It was the artist, not the actress, who spoke and moved...; not the accomplished elocutionist, but one who felt every word...and threw her whole soul into the beautiful imagery, the intense pathos, or the grim tragedy of the lines.
>
> (27 December 1904)

Privately, Gerald Marr Thompson, a great admirer of Bernhardt's confided, "We were charmed. During the evening I sent in my card under cover with congratulations to Miss Brune."[14]

Her Peter Pan seemed beyond criticism because Williamson had sent her to London where she had observed the original production and received coaching from the author. However, a contributor to *Poverty Point* noted that the Australian production had been turned into a star vehicle by such devices as giving many of Wendy's lines to Peter and leaving Peter on stage alone at the end of the play (*Bulletin*, 17 September 1908).

Her Juliet was problematic. Every critic said that she was good in some scenes, clearly implying that she was not so good in others, but there was no consensus on what the good scenes were. Unlike her other roles, she seemed not to have had a coherent idea of the character, but to have played each scene for itself. Thompson was publicly kind, "A highly intelligent reading...emphasising both the gentleness and the youth of the character" (*SMH*, 14 November 1904), but privately he noted, "Miss Brune too small & plain for the part in a frightful fair wig which made her almost ugly. Her balcony scene charming."[15] The *Age* thought her Juliet most distinguished by its "modernity":

> All her little mannerisms, her tricks of gesture and intonation, her portrayal of emotion generally savored of the twentieth century stage—the manifest result of her histrionic upbringing. It helped her materially in such situations as the potion scene, where a singleness of sentiment had to be emphasised with all the power at her command; but when it came to the swift changes of temperament so marked in Juliet, that same training cramped the spacious greatness of Shakespeare's genius.
>
> (23 January 1905)

Criticism of her Dorothy Vernon, a *Romeo and Juliet* story set in Elizabethan times, gives a clearer indication of her essentially modern quality. While finding her "piquant and high spirited, imperious and tender in turn," the *Age* thought that "at only one point did she lose touch. ...A girl of Dorothy Vernon's upbringing would never have pounded on the door in an agony of apprehension" (15 April 1906). The *Argus* agreed that "she presents...a thoroughly modern go ahead heroine full of vivacity" (16 April 1906).

Her one clear failure was as Kundry in *Parsifal*. Thomas Hilhous Taylor had conceived the role with her in mind, and over her own objections, Williamson insisted she play it.[16] She had satisfied audiences as Theodora, Cleopatra, and Tosca, all of whom had tempted and seduced, she had a trained singing voice, and her "serpentine" dance in imitation of Loie Fuller had caused a sensation in 1894. The reviews were tactfully respectful, but the crux seemed to be the scene in which she attempted a striptease. It was not convincing, and the humor of a *Poverty Point* description (reminiscent of Mark Twain's description of Adah Isaacs Menken's *Mazeppa*) may be the most accurate description of the effect:

Gaston Mervale, as Klingsor, commands Kundry to distract holy knight Amfortas' attention, while he (Klingsor) grabs the sacred spear. "Disrobe, Kundry," he says. I woke and thought things were livening up, "Boo!" says Tittell Kundry Brune in a heartrending tone (don't know what she means). "Dis-ah-r-r-r-robe Kundry!" And Kundry does nineteen, slow, careful poses with a green cloak and puts it carefully on the floor—Klingsor waiting so patiently and politely, poor man, and Amfortas presumably kicking his mailed heels on the mat. Then comes a little red over-skirt. Then, very reluctantly, Kundry takes off her necklace and stands forth in—keep calm!—a thick, bunchy white dress from the collar-bones to the elbows and toes! It did not even cling, and the merest man could tell that there were corsets and suspenders and all sorts of bulky flannel-ette things underneath. ...It is disappointing to have one's feelings harrowed up, and then to be confronted by a lady in warm sensible clothes and a bath robe.

("J. E. M", *Bulletin*, 11 April 1907:9)

Compared to Cora Potter and Nance O'Neil, Minnie Tittell Brune was a child, not a woman, a tease, not a temptress.

At the end of her engagement, she found great success as her namesake, Minnie, in *The Girl of the Golden West*, a part in which she seemed to combine most successfully her childlike larrikin with her passionate woman. The reviews dwelt at length on the power of the primitive setting and the distinctively American quality of the pioneer experience, but at heart, they seemed to see a disguised toga play in which the ideal of pure womanhood redeemed sinful man. As the *Argus* said, "The business...is to portray the essential innocence, purity, self-respect, and influence for good of an uneducated, true-hearted girl" (29 March 1909).

One cannot help but be struck by the irony that while both Cora Potter and Minnie Tittell Brune were slender, the one was seen as a decidedly feminine seductress, while the other was not. Minnie succeeded more as a man or a man's mate than she did as the object of a man's sexual desire. Her androgynous persona suggests the emergence of a new gender role. Though female, she appears male. Thus she can engage in social and physical actions that are conventionally masculine without outraging the audience's values, while, at the same time, because she is female, she can revert at a moment's need to that role. In this way, the actress presents the Modern Woman who combines male and female virtues.

Although Gerald Marr Thompson thought she was really only "a good stock actress," she improved.[17] Even her severest critic, *The Bulletin*, acknowledged in 1907 that, "She used to be too explosive—remember how she...generally ramped round in '*L'Aiglon*'? She has dropped that, and is acting with more brains" (21 February 1907). Retrospectively "O.K.," a regular contributor to *Poverty Point* may have said it best:

The wonder was that she so often scored a considerable success, and so rarely made a distinct failure. Tittell Brune had nothing but her cleverness, her alertness and her comparative youthfulness...to account for her popularity...She was just a character actress, full of intelligence and "go."

(*Bulletin*, 10 February 1910:9)

After Australia, she joined her husband in London where she replaced Irene Vanbrugh as Clair Forster in *The Woman in the Case*. They made England their home, and she continued to act until 1923.

As an indication of local approval, she and Nance O'Neil were the two American performers who were memorialized in an historical tableau that concluded the final performance given at Her Majesty's Theatre, Sydney, in 1933 (*SMH*, 12 June 1933).

CHAPTER 10

The American Idiom: Miners and Gals

THE EFFECT OF THE CHANGES DESCRIBED in Chapter 8 were apparent in two plays about the Australian bush: George Darrell's *The Sunny South* (1883), and Alfred Dampier's and Garnett Walch's dramatization of Rolf Bolderwood's novel, *Robbery Under Arms* in 1890.[1] Moreover, these successes were built on a foundation of American players of American plays about the frontier.

The new element was to be found in the representation of the California mining frontier typified by the stories of Bret Harte and Mark Twain. Dr. Neild carefully outlined what he understood to be the differences between the Australian and the American miner. The latter:

> Seems to be more under the influence of the scenes which surround him and the work which occupies him. These two agencies appear to have controlled his nature so completely, that he may be regarded as a genuine product of the soil. His habits, his manners, his language are all coloured thereby.
>
> (*Australasian*, 11 October 1879)

One can infer that the Australian miner, therefore, retained a distinct British character and culture in spite of his surroundings.

A group of expatriate Americans first presented Harte's world in Australia. In the order of their arrival, they were Mr. and Mrs. Frank M. Bates, R. D'Orsay Ogden, Mr. and

Mrs. Thomas J. Herndon, James J. Wallace, Theodore Hamilton, and William H. Leake. They were refugees from a rapidly changing American theatre. Theatrical business was blighted by the national depression of 1878, and all but a handful of resident theatrical companies disbanded. Theatres increasingly relied on companies assembled in New York City and sent on national tour. These were called "combination" companies, and while some played small repertories, most offered only a single play.

Either unable or unwilling to find places in such companies, these actors seem to have come to Australia in an attempt to maintain their traditional pattern of working. They supported major stars in the cities and toured smaller places as stars themselves as they had in America. They seem to have known or known of each other. During most of 1879 and 1880, they played at the Princess's Theatre (renamed the People's) in Melbourne. For about twelve months, the theatre was an American outpost. Its representations of gold-rush America seem to have been popular. Their prices of admission were about half that of the competing Theatre Royal, whose manager, George Coppin, estimated their weekly gross at £200 and cut his prices accordingly.[2]

Since Ogden and Leake remained in Australia, they are the most important of this group, but the others deserve brief notice. Mr. and Mrs. Frank M. Bates came to Australia for two tours. The first lasted from 4 August 1873 through 7 September 1874, the second from 19 February 1877 to 17 June 1879. They offered an unusually large repertory because she was an emotional actress and he was a Yankee specialist. They were more often seen in Boucicault's *The Octoroon* than in any other piece. She was Zoe, the Octoroon, while he was the Yankee overseer, Salem Scudder. Most frequently, though, she was the feature as the emotional center of *The Flowers of the Forest*, *East Lynne*, *Frou-Frou*, or *The French Pocket Book*.

On their second visit, they also attempted Shakespeare, but neither had the requisite voice or physique. Dismissed in Sydney and tolerated in Melbourne, their classical efforts were best received during a season of over 150 nights in Brisbane. Of *Richard III*, the *Courier* said:

> Mr. Bates...acted with much spirit, and was deservedly well received; while...Mrs. Bates occasionally reminded one of first-class acting. ...Notwithstanding a few...weaknesses, and some anachronisms in the way of costume, the whole representation was exceedingly creditable.
>
> (25 June 1877)

The paper recorded the gratitude of the community for Bates's eight months of management "in the face of considerable difficulties" (22 January 1878).

Bates was found dead in Melbourne on 27 June 1879, stripped of his valuables. In his capacity as Assistant Coroner, Dr. Neild determined that he had died of a heart attack (*Age*, 28 and 30 June). Though bereaved, Mrs. Bates continued to act until late November when she returned to the States. A regular performer in San Francisco, she devoted much of her time to encouraging their daughter, Blanche, who became a prominent actress in the United States at the turn of the century.

Hamilton was a reliable actor in New York City, supporting Edwin Booth as Claudius and Macduff in 1870. After returning from Australia, he continued to act until 1905 in a variety of popular plays. Wallace, likewise, was a regular strong supporting player in New York during the 1870s, eventually writing his own starring vehicle. Mr. and Mrs. Herndon played Salem Scudder and Zoe (*The Octoroon*) most often when starring on their own, but they were strictly supporting players at the People's Theatre.

D'Orsay Ogden was himself a character out of Harte's fiction. As Richard Wesley, he played minor roles in the Ohio Valley in 1855, but as D. Ogden, he acted in Nashville in 1859 and was a member of the Richmond Theatre company in 1861. Later in Australia, he claimed that he had fought for the Confederacy with honor, achieving the rank of Colonel and being wounded at the battle of Malvern (*DM*, 3 April 1899).

The facts were otherwise. Ordered to report for military service, he twice escaped from custody and was finally sentenced to three months as a hospital orderly.[3] He made his first appearance in New York City in March 1867 and acted there and in the American South for the next ten years. On 16 February 1878, he began starring as Sandy in Bret Harte's *Two Men of Sandy Bar*, based on Harte's friendship with Mark Twain, in Melbourne. With the exception of a visit to California in 1890, he remained in Australia.

He married the young actress Helen Fergus during a tour of New Zealand in 1879, and from this point on, his efforts were on management of his own company, which eventually featured Baby Ogden, billed as Miss Beatrice. Through the 1880s, the Ogdens alternated long tours, which included Australian country towns, New Zealand, India, and Hong Kong, with periods of residence in Melbourne where he taught acting and gave performances with his students in suburban town halls (*Bulletin*, 13 February 1892).

In October of 1892, he moved to Sydney where he continued to fill professional engagements, most notably as Pistol in Rignold's *Henry V* (September 1894). From the premises of Protestant Hall (238 Castlereagh Street) he offered "thorough Instruction in Elocution, Voice-building, Dramatic Art Generally" (*SMH*, 19 April 1902) and performed with his students at the Royal Standard Theatre, as well as at suburban public halls (*Telegraph*, 8 November

1897; *SMH*, 1–17 October 1898). He took "farewell" benefits in 1899, 1902, and 1904. In the last instance, he wrote Gerald Marr Thompson that he needed the money because his students owed him £100. Thompson had attended the earlier benefit, which he characterized as "a dud," and he didn't puff this one.[4] Ogden disappeared after supporting Minnie Tittell Brune in New Zealand during 1905. Helen Fergus remained in Sydney, and Baby Ogden became the actor Nellie Fergusson.

Ogden's acting in rough and drunken parts was widely approved. The two roles for which he was noted were Sandy in *Two Men of Sandy Bar* and Bill Sykes. Of the former, Dr. Neild said, "He made the picturesque roughness conspicuous without introducing any coarseness. He let the manliness shine through the drunkenness. His degradation, although it had lowered him, had not deprived him of his self-respect" (*Australasian*, 23 February 1878). Of the latter, Dr. Neild thought that "Mr. Ogden is to be credited with a high measure of artistic skill and genuine dramatic feeling for the way in which he worked out the character. It was terrible, but it was probable. His last scene was tragic" (*Australasian*, 6 May 1878). The other role for which he was highly regarded was that of a Mexican outlaw in *The Miner's Daughter*. The *Adelaide* review is typical: "D'Orsay Ogden is deserving of high praise for his make-up and acting in the part of…Pedro Walter. It was a carefully-studied effort, and his cold-blooded villainy earned for him a hearty round of groans at the end of each act" (*Advertiser*, 10 October 1888). He was also adept at broad comedy. His Pistol was a "delightful" character, "who swashed it with heroic bravery" (*Telegraph*, 11 September 1894), and he appeared successfully with both Kelly and Leon's Minstrels (October–November 1880) and Harry Rickards's variety company (October 1890).

William H. Leake was the best type of American actor. After twenty years in stock companies and touring combinations in support of stars, he sought a place in the theatrical heavens where he might shine. His playing of Shakespeare was described in Chapter 8. Here the concern is with his representation of the idiomatic American in the guise of a gold miner. Unquestionably the most successful of all gold rush plays, *My Partner* is apt to strike a modern audience as one more old-fashioned melodrama: The villain murders a miner and frames the dead man's partner for the deed. From the scaffold, the innocent man offers to marry the heroine, who has borne a child fathered by the dead man. The comic Chinaman discovers evidence of the villain's guilt, justice is served, and honor restored. Therefore, it is good to begin by noting that the *Herald* found the play "a plain, unvarnished tale, quietly and consistently told" (1 November 1880). Moreover, it found Leake "an actor of very superior powers," who infused his part with "vivid touches of nature and traits of delicate realism," and found "rare force…in the honesty and straightforward earnestness which marked his bearing." His playing of the role was received equally well in Melbourne. The *Age* approved of the story because it did not depict the "rough, lawless and rude" aspects of the gold fields, but rather that aspect of the society in which "the refining influence of a woman's love has cast its spell" (7 March 1881).

There were dissenting opinions. Dr. Neild would have none of the play. Despite his earlier liking for *The Danites*, he could not now accept the exaltation of "some rough miner to the position of a demigod" (*Australasian*, 12 March 1881), but he did approve of Leake's restrained acting. The *Hobart Mercury* thought "its American origin is stamped too plainly upon it to make it a great favourite. …It is evidently written for a Yankee audience, and that is a great drawback" (18 January 1881), but as the *Advertiser* noted:

The rough elements of camp life in the gold-fields…are not attractive subjects in the eyes of some of our playgoers, but they are not the less actually representative of one section of humanity with which many of our readers are familiar, and in the goldfields history of the sister colonies more than one parallel might easily be found.

(13 June 1881)

A stock character of Bret Harte's stories was the American girl or "gal," a female Huck Finn who fit the Australian notion of a larrikin. Uncorseted in costume and manner, she was an appealing alternative to the feminine domestic saint of middle class orthodoxy.[5] Lotta Crabtree had created this American idiomatic version of the traditional soubrette, and Amy Stone, "Little Nell, the California Diamond," Katie Putnam, Carrie Swain, and Maggie Moore all played her in Australia.

H. F. and Amy Stone appeared in Melbourne during April 1875, and then had a long season from 26 July to 12 November in Sydney. He was most successful in eccentric comic parts, replacing George Fox as Gumption Cute in the original production of *Uncle Tom's Cabin*. She was most successful in roles that were melodramatic extensions of the traditional soubrette: *Fanchon and Cigarette*. It was in the multiple roles of the latter that she appeared most often in Australia. The newspapers dismissed her as a serious actress; however, they grudgingly admired her energy and varied talents in larrikin roles, "She sings, and plays very fairly on the cornet and upon the drum, and, in broadsword practice, she is clever enough to raise a tumult in pit and gallery" (*Argus*, 5 April 1875). The significance of Amy Stone's performances is that they introduced this type of character to Australian audiences, a type that American actresses would make increasingly popular.

No sooner had the Stones ceased than "Nell" commenced. She starred in a version of *Little Nell and the Marchioness* and in *Fidelia the Fire Waif*, a protean vehicle in which she played half a dozen parts and both genders. Characterizing Fidelia as "the veriest nightmare of pistolling, booting, stabbing, house burning, dancing, singing, and banjo playing," the *Argus* paid tribute to her abilities as a variety performer of "great vigour and abandon" and noted that she would have been popular with the audiences of Bret Harte's communities (22 November 1875). The *Age* noted that she was a favorite with the "more demonstrative" members of the Melbourne audience (23 November 1875). She played twice as many performances in Sydney as in Melbourne. Acknowledging the nature of her material, the *Herald* noted that the house was crowded and that her musical numbers were encored.

After eight months in Australia, Nell went to France where, reportedly on the proceeds from investing in the Comstock mine, she studied and matured. As Helen Dauvrey, she managed New York City's Lyceum Theatre, and scored her greatest success as Kate Shipley in Bronson Howard's *One of Our Girls* (1885), a role she played successfully when she returned to Sydney for seven weeks at the end of 1895.[6] Kate, like Helen Dauvrey, grew up and acquired manners, but she remained the American girl, "light-hearted, independent, sincere, and full of natural humour" (*SMH*, 8 November 1895), a perfect counterpart to the typical Australian girl described by Twopeny:

> Her frankness and good-fellowship are captivating. ...She is rarely affected, and is singularly free from "notions," though by no means wanting in ideas and in conversation of a not particularly cultured description.[7]

Carrie Swain was the most virtuosic of these actresses. Beginning in 1878 as a clog dancer, she moved into the dramatic repertory in 1883 with Leonard Grover's *Cad, the Tomboy*, which Odell dismissed as "unimportant," and which was certainly a failure, drawing no more than $200 a night in a theatre that would hold $1,200.[8] Nevertheless, it was her starring vehicle for the next year and the one she chose to open with in Melbourne on 4 December 1886. She played in Australia and New Zealand for two years, and her repertory was almost exclusively made up of *The Tomboy*, Bret Harte's *The Miner's Daughter*, and *Uncle Tom's Cabin*.

The reviews from Melbourne, Sydney, Adelaide, and Brisbane make it clear that she was the most energetic and physically active performer Australian audiences had seen. Everyone commented on her agility. The difference was whether one thought it appropriate. In reviewing *The Tomboy*, the *Age* did not:

> It ought not to be much of a recommendation to an actress that she can kick a hat off a gentleman's head, nor is it a high class entertainment in which the laughter is mainly provoked by a young girl gamboling about the stage, displaying such disregard of feminine sobriety of motion as ought only to be imagined in connection with savage life.
>
> (6 December 1886)

The *Advertiser* was more moderate:

> While her style is decidedly…American, and on this account perhaps not quite acceptable to the whole of her audience…she is clever…and was called to the footlights at the close of every act. …Her attire is odd, and her movements are outré, but…except for a somewhat free use of her pedal extremities it cannot fairly be said there is anything objectionable in her performance.
>
> (28 December 1887)

Another attribute of her athleticism was her ability to swim. For her final Melbourne season, the Theatre Royal filled up the water tank for *The Tomboy*. To rescue a drowning child, she did a swan dive into the water, swam out to some rocks, retrieved the "baby" and swam back, spitting water from between her teeth (*Bulletin*, 16 June 1888).

It was in Sydney that she first did *Mab, The Miner's Daughter*, based on the characters of Bret Harte's story *M'liss*. (Based on character names and plot synopsis, Carrie Swain's play was almost certainly Clay Greene's *M'liss*.) The *Herald*'s notice suggests that as Mab she created something altogether different and more memorable than she had done before:

> Miss Swain was quaint and original; her pathos rang true, and her humour was most unforced. It is seldom that an audience sees a wayward, true-hearted girl's nature so prettily sketched, and carried out with such artistic fidelity.
>
> (11 April 1887)

The same admiration greeted her in Brisbane. The *Courier* critic noted that her vocal range was "nearly three octaves" (29 September 1887) and praised its use, "Her shakes and trills astonished the audience, and before she had finished the applause was deafening."

The Bulletin's last memory of her may well have been that of her audiences: "a vision of two heels attired in large smashed boots…a delicious cloud of golden hair, a tank, a magnificent voice. …She can hang on to a note longer than any other two ladies we know of" (13 October 1888).

Compared with the success of Amy Stone, Nell, and Carrie Swain, the dismal failure of Katie Putnam can be attributed both to her lack of talent and to weak material. At the age of twelve, she was starring as Pauline in *The Lady of Lyons* (*New York Clipper*, 15 August 1863), and she was a regular touring star in the American West during the 1880s. Her repertory in both countries drew from the same line of prodigious females as the others: *Fanchon*; *The Old Curiosity Shop*; *Erma, the Elf* by Charles T. Dazey; and *Lena the Madcap*, for which she claimed credit.

She was in Australia for slightly more than two months during the latter half of 1889 and gave no more than twelve performances of any of her pieces in Melbourne, Sydney, and Brisbane. The *Bulletin* thought she lacked the "genius" of Maggie Moore and the "voice and vitality" of Carrie Swain (15 June 1889) and concluded: "Katie Putnam's art begins in an Amurriken accent and finishes at sass; directly she can't sass any more her histrionic powers peter out" (22 June 1889).

Given these precedents, it is not surprising that Maggie Moore added the mining camp larrikin to her repertory. She had grown up in a San Francisco that still remembered the glory of its gold rush days. She had doubtless seen Lotta Crabtree perform, and she had long-standing friendships with Clay Greene and McKee Rankin, both of whom specialized in dramatizing Bret Harte's world. The tomboy character suited her abilities while providing some variety in her repertory, and it had already proved popular with the Australian audience.

She and Williamson had performed McKee Rankin's version of Joaquin Miller's play *The Danites in the Sierras* in Melbourne (4 October 1879) and Adelaide (3 May 1880), but they had retired at the centenary of European settlement in Australia. When she resumed playing in July 1890, a great deal had changed both in the country and in her private life. She and Williamson were separated, and he waged a bitter, unsuccessful legal battle to deny her the right to play *Struck Oil*. She divorced him in 1901, marrying her leading man, Harry R. Roberts, the next year. To support herself, she toured all across Australia, appearing as frequently in Brisbane and Perth as in the larger cities. Three times (1900, 1903, and 1907), she toured in America, while Roberts tried to establish himself separately as a leading man. She stopped playing as a star in 1912, although she continued to appear as a featured player as late as 1920. Her final years are noted in Chapter 13.

Struck Oil remained her most popular piece, first with John Forde and then with Roberts as John Stofel. In addition, she could always rely on Boucicault's Irish heroines. However, during the 1890s, she introduced four mining camp larrikin roles into her repertory: the title roles in *Meg, the Castaway* and *M'liss*; Carrots in McKee Rankin's adaptation of Joaquin Miller's *Forty-Nine* ('49); and Bessie Fairfax in Clay Greene's *The Golden Giant Mine*. M'liss served for only a handful of performances during 1892 and 1893, but she played Meg, Carrots, and Bessie until 1909.

The character of the larrikin waif allowed her to display her abilities in song, dance, comedy, and pathos all in one play, and both the character and the gold rush setting were popular with audiences both because they corresponded to the emerging sense of Australian identity and because they adhered to accepted melodramatic conventions. They were all built around the rescue of the innocent, impoverished girl from a villain.

Meg, M'liss, and Carrots were all introduced on an extended country tour between March and October of 1892 that began in Brisbane and finished in Adelaide. The *Courier* approved of *Forty-Nine* because, "There is not a first-class deed of blood...not a single murder, or a shot fired, no fearful deed of villainy or gruesome situation. It is a clean, breezy, and healthy piece" (1 April 1892), and it thought she was "simple, easy, and natural" in *M'liss* (5 April 1892). In Melbourne, the *Age* described her Meg as, "rowdy, quiet, impertinent, reasonable, careless, humorous, pathetic and loving all by turns, and all the time she impresses her audience with her innate goodness" (31 October 1892), but the *Australasian* shrewdly noted that as M'liss, "Miss Moore…does not present the M'liss of the American author, she enacts a character which is highly entertaining from the purely comic point of view, and also attractive in the matter of singing and dancing" (19 November 1892).

She began playing *The Golden Giant* in 1894 during a long season in Melbourne. The *Age*, as always, found, "Her representation of the 'tom-boy' was perfectly natural; there was nothing exaggerated, nothing studied or set" (25 June 1894), and the *Advertiser* congratulated the playwright for having "written a play dealing with mining in America without the aide of sudden death or murder" (25 February 1895). As late as 1910, playing the piece under the title *The Gambler's Sweetheart*, she received the ultimate accolade: "Maggie Moore…played the character…with a vivacity and archness reminiscent of her never-to-be-forgotten Lizzie Stofel" (5 December 1910). The truth was, audiences came to see Maggie Moore play Maggie Moore, regardless of accent or national setting. She got fat, her voice faded, but she still epitomized the larrikin spirit of an audience that regarded itself as descended from convicts, bush rangers, miners, shearers, and jackaroos. As the *Argus* observed at the very end of her career:

> The homely humour of the Stofel home is based upon a human reality, and it is this quality of humanity which keeps *Struck Oil* alive. …There are some eternal truths which must be understood before one's education is complete—*Hamlet*, *Traviata*, *The Silver King*,…*Sydney Harbour*, and Miss Maggie Moore as Lizzie Stofel.
>
> (1 September 1913)

It is significant that the characters of the American miner and the female larrikin, and the actors who played them, were treated respectfully and sympathetically by Australian reviewers and were apparently popular with Australian audiences. The terms of approval were essentially the same as those extended to Jefferson's Yankees. A lack of middle-class manners in dress, speech, or stage business did not automatically bar one from admission to the parlor. The audience believed (or wished to believe) that they were tolerant enough to judge a person's character by more significant choices in life. So long as one practiced the virtues of hard work and honesty, so long as one was loyal and brave, one was accepted. Clearly there was a style of acting that came to be associated with these characters. Generally, the actors were subdued. That is, they played the character for consistency rather than for momentary effect. They were also absorptive, not reflective, inviting the audience to participate with them rather than being dazzled by them. Even Carrie Swain, otherwise, one suspects, a reflective performer, dazzling in her athleticism, seems to have become subdued and absorptive in her portrayal of Mab. Thus in character and performance, the idiomatic characters of the California gold rush era resonated with an audience that was gradually defining itself as Australian.

CHAPTER 11

The Soldier, the Cowboy, and the Renewal of a Culture

IT SEEMS CLEAR from the Australian careers of the players studied in the two previous chapters that after 1890, America became an increasing source of new ideas, products, and energy in the construction of Australian culture. As Will Rogers observed about Australians:

> Anything new or what they haven't had before will be called American. You hear electric street cars called American tram cars. All the refreshment places are advertised in box car letters "American cold Drinks American Soda fountain ["] the bars will have up drinks mixed on the American plan. The barber will advertise "American barber chair" [sic].[1]

Yet the origins of American innovation at the turn of the twentieth century arose during a crisis of confidence in the United States that stemmed, ironically, from its success. In claiming its own empire (Hawaii, Cuba, and the Philippines), the United States had violated what had previously been regarded as the sacred rule of George Washington's farewell advice to avoid foreign entanglements. Insecure in its new role of international power, the nation was also troubled at home. The long reign of post-Civil War prosperity ended in the depression that began in 1890, and immigrants continued to pour into Eastern cities at the same time as the Bureau of the Census declared that the

Western frontier, traditionally the destination of migrants, no longer existed.

One cultural response to this challenge was the rise of spontaneous, assertive behavior, reflected in the rise of outdoor recreation (sports, cycling, hiking, swimming) as an alternative to the genteel tradition. The United States pinned its hopes on the man of action.[2] As latter-day knights errant, the soldier and the frontiersman were expected to bring reforming values forged on the frontiers of savagery back to the centers of civilization. A descendent of the Yankee character adapted to other frontiers, this character was now symbolized by the cowboy and the soldier as personified by Theodore Roosevelt, who had been both.

A near-sighted asthmatic graduate of Harvard, who loved exercise and gloried in physical challenge, he emerged from three years of part-time ranching in the Badlands of North Dakota, a tough, forceful champion of rugged individualism.[3] His writings celebrated the regenerative force of the strenuous life, and his career, from his military accomplishments in Cuba to the presidency, affirmed its effectiveness. Roosevelt's experience, elaborated by the stories of Owen Wister and the art of Frederick Remington, both of whom claimed to have been similarly reborn in the West, combined with military images from the Civil War and Indian Wars into America's icon of the savior of Western Civilization. As Roosevelt described him:

> Meanness, cowardice, and dishonesty are not tolerated. There is a high regard for truthfulness and keeping one's word, intense contempt for any kind of hypocrisy, and a hearty dislike for a man who shirks his work. ...A cowboy will not submit tamely to any insult, and is ever ready to avenge his own wrongs; nor has he an overwrought fear of shedding blood. He possesses...to a very

high degree, the stern, manly qualities that are invaluable to a nation.[4]

Many of these qualities were familiar to Australians. The soldier was the most familiar representation of the new hero. British drama had a vigorous tradition of military melodrama, and William Gillette's two Civil War plays were popular in Australia. *Held by the Enemy* was produced there between 1887 and 1915, and *Secret Service* was played about half as often between 1899 and 1903. *Secret Service* offered a particularly American version of the military hero. Instead of a protagonist distinguished by feats of arms, Gillette's play offered one distinguished by mental quickness. As a spy, Louis Dumonte necessarily acted alone, thus perpetuating the particularly American penchant for the individual who, when necessary, acts outside the structures of law and society. Dumont is Hawkeye or Davey Crockett in a different setting. Thus Gillette's plays contributed to the representation of the new hero.

It was, however, in the more familiar guise of the frontiersman and cowboy that the American version of the man of action rooted itself in Australian culture at the turn of the century. During the 1870s, Australia developed its own local color melodrama dealing with convicts and bushrangers. Beginning with Walter Cooper's *Foiled*, the genre grew to maturity with Alfred Dampier's adaptation of Rolf Bolderwood's *Robbery Under Arms*. In addition to his original plays of local color, Anglo-Australian actor George Darrell performed Frank Murdoch's *Davey Crockett* under the titles of *Rube Redmond* and *The Deerslayer*, while Sierra mining camp melodrama continued to be played on the Australian stage by Maggie Moore and Minnie Tittell Brune alongside dramas set on the Australian gold fields.[5]

The cowboy frontier shared much the same population of honest working men, noble women, and propertied villains as these other forms, but it added the indigenous native. America's tradition of dealing with American Indians was a double helix: two strands that wound around each other. One strand was real, in which war and removal kept American Indians from interfering with the occupation of land by European immigrants. The other strand was fiction in which American Indians were depicted as noble savages destined to disappear in the tide of universal cultural evolution.

Australians were familiar with the earliest expressions of the fictional strand. Many had read or heard of the stories of James Fenimore Cooper, and almost all had seen a performance of Buckstone's *The Green Bushes*, which put Cooper's Indians on stage. The play was a staple of the Australian repertory up to the early 1870s. Sydney and Melbourne audiences had also seen productions of both Louisa Medina's *Nick of the Woods* and Robert Montgomery Bird's *Metamora*. However, the most prominent expressions of the traditional American attitude toward its indigenous peoples came in the cowboy melodramas and Wild West shows that flourished in the years surrounding Federation. In the context of the developing policy of a White Australia, it seems reasonable to infer that many Australians shared the American view of the American Indian as a representative of all people of color.

The first American melodramas to exploit the cowboy frontier were *Across the Continent* by Oliver Doud Byron, and *Horizon* by Augustin Daly. The former was played frequently during the 1870s and 1880s in Australia, while there was a single production of the latter in Melbourne during 1879. Both were received as conventional sensation melodramas, and the frontier setting was regarded as a peculiarly American phenomenon. The *Mercury* solemnly intoned that *Across the Continent*:

embraces a narrative founded on fact in connection with the times when life and property were much more insecure than they are now in some parts of the United States, though that is not saying a lot, for as we all know, things are far from what they should be "Out West," even at the present day.

(9 October 1893)

The Wild West show grew out of America's fascination with the character of Buffalo Bill, who was constructed by Ned Buntline (E. Z. C. Judson) from the exploits of William F. Cody. While Cody appeared in these melodramas, he was a wretched actor, and it was difficult to include his skills at riding and shooting on the stage of the average theatre. Consequently, Cody concocted the Wild West show in 1882. It reached its final form at Madison Square Garden four years later as *The Drama of Civilization*, using a script by Steele MacKaye which organized the display of Indian ceremonies, riding, roping, shooting, and mock battles to demonstrate the inevitable triumph of Western civilization.[6]

Since Australia possessed a vast cattle frontier, cowboys (jackaroos), and aboriginal natives, it is not surprising that the American form of entertainment was popular or that there were local versions of it. Indeed, Nat Salsbury (associated with Cody in the conception and management of his show) claimed to have first thought of the idea when witnessing feats of horsemanship in Australia where he toured as a performer during 1877–1878.[7] Representations of the American cowboy frontier arrived in Australia at the beginning of the 1890s with W. F. "Doc" Carver's *Wild America* and the *Wirth Brothers Wild West Show*. The Wirths returned to Australia and New Zealand from 1899 through 1904, competing at the turn of the century with Texas Jack's show, which for a short time featured Will Rogers as the Cherokee Kid. Local performers called "Broncho Bob" and

"Broncho George" were active with their own shows in the first few years of the twentieth century.

The Wild West show was usually organized around a narrative of Indian raid and cowboy retaliation, so the form lent itself and its performers to more conventional theatrical exploitation. Alfred Dampier and Garnett Walch quickly concocted two vehicles for Dampier's daughter, *Lily*, and *Doc Carver: The Scout and The Trapper*. The former was more successful, and its script survives.

The Scout was described by the *Bulletin* as "a wild aquatic hippodrome in four acts, ten yells, three plunges and a piercing shriek" (23 May 1891). The heiress heroine is the lustful object for both a crooked lawyer and an Indian, who conspire to abduct her, but she is rescued by her true love, the scout. The events that caused the greatest excitement were in the second scene of the second act. Carver and Lily escape from the Indian camp on horseback across a bridge. She crosses safely, but the bridge collapses under him, plunging his horse into the water fifteen feet below while he saves himself by grasping hold of the broken span (*Argus*, 11 May 1891). The only thing that saved the rest of the play from anti-climax was the final obligatory struggle between Carver and the villain, which ends with the latter being hurled from a cliff into the water below.[8]

The play was revived as *The Prairie King* for King Hedley in Sydney in 1895 and 1897. Both times, the water tank proved a hazard. On opening night of the first revival, Hedley lost his grip and wound up in the tank, while on the opening night of the second revival, the tank burst just before the curtain rose, and the audience was forced to wait while it was patched and refilled. While Hedley was presented as an American, he was born in Bairnsdale, Victoria, and he was said to have worked as a mounted policeman and as a journalist before succumbing to the lure of the stage in the United States (*The Golden Age*, 26 February 1897). He acted at San Francisco's Baldwin Theatre from 1878 to 1880, playing the Apostle Peter in Salmi Morse's *Passion Play.*[9] The company of that theatre was perhaps the best regional stock company in America at the time. Hedley learned his craft from its leading actors, James O'Neill, Lewis Morrison, and James A. Herne, and from its young resident playwright, David Belasco. When not acting, he participated in athletic contests that offered cash prizes. In an account of one of them, he was described as "27 years old, 6 feet, 163 pounds" (*Alta,* 2 October 1879). In August of 1880, he went east, and from 1885 to 1895 appeared in major melodramatic roles.

The *Telegraph*'s reviewer characterized his acting in melodrama as: "of the quiet and calm school, the primary belief of which is that the actor acts for himself, and disregards the audience. …In America, as we know, it is the latest idea" (7 October 1895), continuing: "Mr. Hedley…never tries to drive home 'points,' and he plays away from his audience all the time, ignoring them. …This may or may not do here, but the artistic merit…is unquestionable" (28 October 1895). Other notices were ambivalent. While they generally approved of his restraint, they also noted that he was wooden in action and often inaudible. Clearly, what they understood to be the new American style of acting confused them. In theory, it was admirable, but in Hedley's practice, it was not. His last Australian performances were in Melbourne during September and October of 1898. Most of his notices were positive; there had clearly been an adjustment. Some time afterwards, he went to England where he acted and was reported to have married a wealthy widow (*Bulletin,* 24 January 1903).

Australian audiences got their next exposure to the American man of action and the newer style of acting between May and September 1903. The Frawley-Neill company was organized by James Neill around the actor T.

Daniel Frawley, who had been a stock leading man in San Francisco. Since 1895, he had headed his own company, which played all over the country but was especially popular on the Pacific Coast.

Their Pacific engagements began at Manila on 15 September 1902 and were unsuccessful because, "Manila, Yokohama and the seaport cities of India and China are all but crowded with American theatrical enterprises" (*DM*, 28 March 1903). While playing in Calcutta, they were engaged by Williamson. For their Australian season, Frawley remained the leading man with young Mary Van Buren as his leading lady, a position she had filled for five years. However, the company was augmented by Susie Vaughn, a strong English character actor from the company of Robert Brough, and by Harrington Reynolds, an Englishman, who had acted with Frawley in the United States. They opened in Melbourne on 30 May 1903 in *Secret Service*. From then until 29 September in Melbourne, Sydney, and Brisbane, they offered eight plays. Augustus Thomas's *Arizona* was most popular, played twice as often as *Secret Service*, the next most popular piece. In Sydney and Brisbane, they also presented the Western cavalry drama *The Girl I Left Behind Me* by Franklin Fyles and David Belasco and Thomas's rural American comedy *In Mizzoura*. The former was received as a typical military melodrama, while the latter will be discussed in Chapter 12.

They were well-received because of the restrained style of their acting. The *Australasian* described the hallmarks of Frawley's acting as, "repose, restraint, refinement," noting that, "at times he underkeyed the rendering slightly...but he quickly gauged the ear of the house afresh" (1 June 1903). The *Bulletin* described Mary Van Buren as "a buxom charmer, with an hour-glass figure" (6 June 1903), while the *Argus* thought she "played with easy naturalness and studied quietness" (1 June 1903).

The *Bulletin* thought *Arizona* "good, reasonable melodrama, introducing touches of Yankee novelty, and new workings of old effects" (27 June 1903), while the *Australasian* noted that "the picturesque delineation of ranch life in the Far West gives the production the flavour that audiences look for in typical American drama" (27 June 1903).

Opinion was not unanimous about the acting. The *Age* cautioned that "the repressed style...may easily be overdone, leading...the audience to suspect an actor of internal fires of passion which he may not possess" (22 June). The *Telegraph* contented itself with a fair description of the style of both writing and playing: "There is an absence of effort for effect; intense dramatic situations are briskly carried through without the raising of a voice; all is earnestness and intensity" (13 July). In its notice of *The Girl I Left Behind Me*, the *Courier-Mail* made its approval obvious in a similar description:

> Mr. Frawley and Miss Van Buren avoided conspicuous positions and those old stage tricks which have always been regarded as "the right of the star." They are never obtrusive, they do not attempt to work up "situations."
>
> (21 September 1903)

Despite such general approval and newspaper assurances of popularity, the company did only fair business in Australia, which its members attributed to drought and labor unrest. They were, however, lavish in their praise of Australian hospitality (*DM*, 5 November 1904).

The cowboy frontier was not fully integrated with the emerging local dramas until the arrival of a company engaged by Williamson to play *The Squaw Man* by E. M. Royle and *The Virginian* by Owen Wister and Kirke LaShelle. The company was in Australia for a year (7 July 1906 to 5 July 1907). A blend of American and Anglo-

Australian talent, its leading players were Charles Waldron and Ola Jane Humphrey. Waldron (*Wyngate* and *The Virginian*) was the son of Mr. and Mrs. George Waldron, long-time leading stock players on the Pacific Coast. He became a Broadway leading actor in Belasco's *The Warrens of Virginia* (1909). Humphrey had also begun in West Coast stock, and she remained in Australia for two years after this company disbanded, supporting Julius Knight in *The Scarlet Pimpernel* and *The Prisoner of Zenda* and (after Margaret Anglin's departure) Henry Kolker in *An Englishman's Home*. Among the others, Hardee Kirkland played the most important parts: the Indian chief Tabwana in *The Squaw Man* and the villain Trampas in *The Virginian*.

The stage director and player of the villain Cash Hawkins in *The Squaw Man* was returned Australian actor George Bryant. A native of Victoria, he acted in small roles with Williamson's Royal Dramatic Company, and with Brough and Boucicault from 1886 to 1890. A year later, he was in the United States. After supporting E. H. Sothern and Virginia Harned in costume romance from 1896 to 1901, he played college president Peter Witherspoon in George Ade's comedy, *The College Widow* (1904–1905). He remained in Australia, acting in plays and films, eventually founding Bryant's Theatre with his daughter Beryl in Sydney (1932). Other performers familiar to Australian audiences were Mrs. G. W. B. Lewis, Florence Gleeson (who played Nat-u-rich, daughter of Tabwana), Cyril Mackaye, Harry Plimmer, Fred Cambourne, and George Carey.

Charles Waldron, in particular, continued the restrained style. The *Advertiser* said, "Waldron...is tall, easy, and graceful in his movements, and has a beautifully-modulated voice. ...Above all, he is natural. Mr. Waldron rightly disdains the limelight. He never makes declamatory appeal to the 'gods'" (3 September 1906). Only the *Bulletin* demurred. Its Sydney correspondent thought, "Waldron…represents the Cow-avenger as a cool, calm ice-berg…and if he would thaw…it would be a little relief" (15 November 1906), and his Melbourne colleague agreed: "Up to a certain point his handsome appearance and pleasing manner may be said to play the part excellently. Beyond that point he acts tamely. He takes no risks" (6 June 1907).

Opinion was even more divided about Humphrey. The *Argus* thought, "The complete artistic success…fell to Miss Ola Humphrey as…Molly Wood…Gathering the flying threads, she knotted them in her own personality, creating a veritable human being" (3 June 1907), while the *Bulletin*'s Sydney reviewer thought she had "the same voice, the same staccato delivery" as Nance O'Neil, but without the passion (27 September 1906). His Melbourne colleague dismissed her performance in *The Virginian* as, "hopelessly artificial. She is always the stage lady—charmingly decorative, but not a bit convincing" (6 June 1907). Reviews of her performances in costume romances were unanimously favorable, which suggests that she was more comfortable in a more traditional style.

Players of smaller roles were also singled out by various papers for praise. Commentators were generally impressed with Hardee Kirkland's Tabwana and Rapley Holmes's Big Bill. Of the former, the *Argus* thought "The Indian he depicts is a real Indian—stoical, taciturn, and unemotional" (9 July 1906), while of the latter the *Courier-Mail* thought "Mr. Rapley's Big Bill…was the incarnation of pluck, loyalty, and true mateship" (1 April 1907). However, it was George Bryant who made the greatest impression. The West Australian observed that, "Mr. George Bryant's sketch of Cash…may be true to Western American life; it was certainly violent enough for anything" (5 May 1907). A better idea of Bryant's playing can be gathered from a later contribution to *Poverty Point*:

George Bryant is said to be another of the mummers who take it as a grievance that they are rarely if ever cast for virtuous character parts. ...But Bryant has only his voice to blame. He has cultivated that sonorous, explosive organ to a deep pitch of disrespectability. His accents are bloodthirsty, and his sneer is full of guilt. No man was ever quite so alarming as George Bryant sounds. His bitter laughter threatens sudden death.

("O. K.", Bulletin, 13 May 1915)

Apart from the growing trend toward more absorptive acting, the stories of the plays presumably connected with the audience. In *Arizona*, a woman is saved from the folly of infidelity by a young army officer's lie, even though it places him in a compromising situation. Forced to resign his commission, the young man goes to work for a rancher, rises to foreman, and weds the boss's daughter. Explaining his actions, the rancher states the cowboy's creed:

We take a man on here, and ask no questions. We know when he throws his saddle on his horse, whether he understands his business or not. He may be a minister backslidin', or a banker savin' his last lung, or a train-robber on his vacation—we don't care. A good many of our most useful men have made their mistakes. All we care about now is, will they stand the gaff?[10]

Such a story of redemption and social success must have resonated with an Australian audience aware of its convict and immigrant origins.

The Virginian focused on a city girl's successful adaptation to the frontier. Though she and the Virginian are romantically attracted, the schoolteacher, Molly, is uncomfortable on the prairie. She does not understand the rough horseplay and practical joking that is its humor, and she is horrified by the casual violence. Gradually, through living there, she changes. She learns to ride and camp out, she rescues the Virginian when he is shot, and agrees to marry him.

Not only does the play present violence as inherent in a frontier, it also displays the transforming effect of geography on society. Unlike the larrikin females of mining camp melodrama, Molly is no untutored waif, but a sophisticated city girl. On the frontier, she is transformed. That such a transformation seemed realistic to an Australian audience is supported by the similarity between Molly at the end of the play and the Australian female protagonists created by *"Albert Edmunds"* (Edmund Duggan and Bert Bailey): Violet Enderby in *The Squatter's Daughter* (9 February 1907) and Mona Maitland in *The Man from Out Back* (1 May 1909).[11] Clearly, similar situations in similar cultures produced parallel lines of development that reinforced one another in the mind of the Australian audience.

The Squaw Man was by far the most popular cowboy melodrama in either country. The younger brother of a British Earl takes the blame for his brother's malfeasance and emigrates to the American West. There he becomes a successful rancher and protector of the local Indian chief. Barely surviving an attempted assassination, he is nursed back to health by the chief's daughter. Out of gratitude, he marries her, and they have a son. Five years later, he learns that his brother is dead. Both the title and the love of his brother's widow await him. Unwilling to betray his wife, he agrees to send their boy to England as heir. However, the Indian princess kills herself so that her husband is free to resume his rightful place in society.

The *Age* thought its first half, "just plain ordinary melodrama of no particular merit" (9 July 1906). The *Herald* thought it "an English drawing-room comedy-drama of a perfectly stereotyped pattern" (24 September 1906), while the *Argus* dismissed it as "trite sentimentality and heroics usually restricted to the most meretricious melodrama" (9 July 1906). Given these responses, one is puzzled by the play's great popularity. The triumph of British nobility in civilizing the savage was partly responsible, but one suspects that for all the protestations of cultural difference to the contrary, it was rooted in shared attitudes toward non-Anglo-Saxon peoples. The avowedly racist *Bulletin* put it clearly:

> It looks a tough proposition to make a hero out of a member of the old nobility who shares his camp with a lubra and sprinkles half-castes around; but by calling her a squaw instead of a lubra, and the camp a ranch, and dressing her in a cloak of many colors and a milk-pail instead of a blue blanket and a clay-pipe, and making her brothers ask for fire-water instead of ticcapenny, the house not only forgives him, but applauds him vigorously. Thus distance lends enchantment.
>
> (27 September 1906)

In this passage the writer deployed the *Bulletin*'s ironic house style to full effect. The detailed comparison suggests that the audience was not fooled by differences in terminology and costume. The appeal of the play to both Americans and Australians was its claim that indigenous people will voluntarily sacrifice themselves so that the Anglo-Saxons could get on with the project of owning the world.

After 1907, no further imported representations of the American frontier appeared on Australia's stages. Audience demand was fully satisfied by the work of local producers. While William Anderson stuck to strictly Australian places and authors, E. I. Cole and George Marlow included both American and Australian frontiers in their repertories. Cole had been co-proprietor of Texas Jacks's Wild West in Brisbane during December 1899, and four years later pitched the tent of his Bohemian Dramatic Company in a vacant lot near Sydney's Central Railway Station. While the majority of his plays were localized, a significant number were set in the Wild West, the Sierras, or Cuba during the Spanish-American War. Cole fancied himself as Buffalo Bill, affecting a similar appearance and playing Bill's roles in *The Scouts of the Prairie* and *Buffalo Bill*. Until 1910, the Bohemian Company alternated between Sydney and Melbourne. From then until the end of 1915, they were principally in Hobart and Adelaide.

Marlow had his own traveling company after 1910, and he featured plays by British writers based on Bret Harte's stories, such as *The Luck of Roaring Camp* by Benjamin Landeck and *At Cripple Creek* by Hal Reid (*DM*, 21 August 1912). That these plays depended on stereotypical characters and ample violence seems clear. Reviewing the former, the *Argus* thought that "Bret Harte…would scarcely have recognized his famous story. …Revolvers cracked and bowie knives flashed according to the popular impression of the customs of California" (6 February 1911). Admiring a later piece, *The Cowboy and the Squaw*, the *Advertiser* remarked:

> The stock of a gun factory appeared to have been but recently distributed among the populace. …The amount of gunpowder expended would have done honor to a Fourth of July celebration or a typical Guy Fawkes Day. There were numbers of horses, too, which came rushing on the stage at frequent intervals.
>
> (29 September 1913)

Apart from sensationalism, though, these plays seemed to have appealed to the audience's nostalgia for an earlier time, when life was simpler and values clearer. The *Mercury* approved of plays like Cole's *Buffalo Bill* because, "Improbable as they are, they are really full of 'heart interest,' and are wholly free from the objectionable eroticism which forms so marked a feature of the modern 'advanced' play" (27 November 1911).

CHAPTER 12

Bosses and Crooks: The Urban Frontier

A LARGE PART OF AUSTRALIA'S NOSTALGIA for the pastoral life was its concern with urban crime. Although its economy depended on agriculture and mining, activities conducted by small numbers of people living on large, isolated tracts of land, more than half of Australians had always lived in cities. By contrast, for all its burgeoning industrial might, the United States had always been rural. Its interior swallowed immigrants wholesale, so that as late as 1890, half of its people lived in or near settlements of fewer than twenty-five hundred persons. All of that changed by 1900: the frontier vanished, and half of the population lived in cities and towns. As a consequence of this change, the focus of American culture shifted in the years before the Great War to the city as the new frontier: the place of economic opportunity that needed civilizing.

This produced a wave of political revolt. Populism began in the agricultural and mining states of the Great Plains and the Rocky Mountains. It demanded changes that would return these areas to their former position of importance and influence, in spite of their declining population and economy. The protest against change was soon taken up by the urban middle and professional classes under the banner of Progressivism. They, too, resented their loss of political and economic power to economic concentration created by vast and growing monopolies in manufacturing, banking, and railroads. Populists and Progressives wanted an end to the consolidation of economic and political power in the hands of a few and a return to the tradition of individual independence and responsibility that lay at the heart of Jefferson's agrarian myth.[1]

Two variations of melodrama were created that embodied the Populist/Progressive protest. First, there were plays that featured the activities of criminals and police. The protagonists, whether crooks or cops, fought against an economic or political combination that deprived them (and those like them) a place in society. Second, there were plays that dealt directly with the actions of business and monopolies. These were the equivalents of the muckraking journalism and fiction of Upton Sinclair and Ida Tarbell.

Nineteenth-century melodrama had always been about money, property, and theft. Its middle- and lower-class audience had always been interested in wealth, how it was gotten, and how it was preserved. Almost always, the heroine was persecuted by the villain for both sexual and financial gratification. She was lovely and (at least potentially) wealthy. Plays in this vein began with Colman the younger's *The Iron Chest* (1796), and both Buckstone and Jerrold wrote plays of detection for London's Surrey Theatre in the late 1820s.

The first melodrama to introduce the underworld of the professional criminal and the police detective was Taylor's *The Ticket-of-Leave Man*. Yet, the detective, Hawkshaw, is only a secondary character. Boucicault's *After Dark* presents a gentleman who functions as a detective in tracking down the true identity of the principal villain, a convict escaped from Australian transportation. Finally, Wilfred Denver, the reformed gambler and drunkard who is the protagonist of Henry Arthur Jones's *The Silver King*, acts as his own detective, disguising himself to ferret out the plots of professional criminals. These plays were performed frequently in Australia, the last surviving well into the early twentieth century.

At the turn of the twentieth century, however, the emblematic detective was Sherlock Holmes. Cuyler Hastings had played him in William Gillette's *Sherlock Holmes* in the United States during 1900–1901, and Williamson brought him to Australia especially to star in it. While he spoke too rapidly and softly for some (*Argus*, 15 September 1902), most agreed that, "He held an audience's attention in a masterful manner, and was gifted with a fine, musical, magnetic voice" ("O.K." in *Poverty Point*, 22 January 1914). The *Age* described his acting as, "Intensity of feeling combined with quietude and self-restraint in its expression. …He has rarely occasion to raise his voice above a monotone, and he is most impressive when…most subdued" (15 September 1902).

Compared to the new variations on the form, the continuing popularity of traditional urban melodrama was confirmed by the success of Walter Sanford's theatrical company, which followed Daniel Frawley's company to New Zealand and Australia between 1904 and 1906, where they performed twenty-five plays, most of which were urban melodramas of crime and passion and all of which featured the triumph of the poor and powerless over their oppressors. Assessing the company's initial offering, the *Herald* contrasted its style with the "quiet, reserved, and artistic style of acting" practiced by Frawley's company (4 July 1904), while other papers reported crowded, enthusiastic houses.

While traditional melodrama of financial oppression was regarded as universal, the newer plays about bosses and crooks were regarded as peculiarly American, representing circumstances that didn't and shouldn't exist in Australia. Charles Klein's *The Lion and the Mouse* brought America's obsession with wealth to the attention of

Australian audiences, and it introduced them to a new American actress, Katherine Grey.

She had played opposite such stars as James A. Herne, Richard Mansfield, William H. Crane, and Arnold Daly, in both traditional genres and the new drama of Ibsen and Shaw. From the end of January 1910 through June of the following year, she appeared in all six Australian cities in nine plays. *The Lion and the Mouse* was her most frequent piece, with Klein's *The Third Degree* and Eugene Walter's *Paid in Full* each being offered about half as often. She was also successful as both Raina and Louka in Shaw's *Arms and the Man*. The persona that emerged was that of the clever, plucky girl who was determined to fight injustice and wrongdoing against overwhelming odds. For Australian audiences, she was the American version of the New Woman. During her first six months, she played opposite popular English romantic leading man Julius Knight, after which she was paired with the American William Desmond.

The newspapers took *The Lion and the Mouse* in stride, only the *Bulletin* and the *Mercury* demurring at the absurdity of a young girl successfully deceiving and morally influencing a man of such wealth, power, and acumen as John Burkett Ryder (10 March 1910; 1 April 1911). It was the character of Ryder who attracted the most notice. Australian commentary described monopoly and corruption as uniquely American—something alien to Australia. The *Age* thought that "the American millionaire who crushes most things human...is becoming fairly well known" (7 March 1910), but the *Advertiser* noted that, "An Australian who has had no experience of corrupt governments and venal politicians can only surmise that Mr. Charles Klein...knew his subject and was confident of his facts," concluding that the United States is, "the native home of the monstrosity" (28 March 1910). The *Courier-Mail* cautioned that the play might lose some of its force in a country, such as Australia, with no multi-millionaires or gigantic monopolies (26 April 1910).

"Slight in figure, confident in manner, and with a full, effective voice which she is apt to employ in the lower range" (*Telegraph*, 24 January 1910), Katherine Grey was praised in all the notices for her emotional power and her naturalness: "She moved and bore her part…as if she were the actual character" (*Courier-Mail*, 26 April 1910). As the *Mercury* observed, "Miss Katherine Grey…is a fine exponent of the modern intellectual school of acting, with an engaging presence, fine diction, and a first-rate stage voice. There is no staginess about her acting" (1 April 1911).

Australian critics were repelled by her crime dramas.[2] While they could accept the violence of the cowboy frontier as necessary, they rejected it in an urban environment. For Americans, the city was just as much a frontier as any other, while for Australians, it was already civilized by definition. This is one of the clearest cases of Australians using American material to construct their own culture. The American frontier was acceptable, but its cities weren't; but one registers a note of self-defense in these objections. "O.K.", a regular contributor to *Poverty Point* summed up the negative feeling:

> My disrespect for the United States…must be rooted, I guess, in a contempt for modern 'Murkan melodrama and comedy. All the recent successes from the U.S. are stories of crime and criminals, the "wrong 'uns," as a rule, being glorified at the expense of the police.
>
> (*Bulletin*, 3 December 1914)

Charles Klein's *The Third Degree* was the first to draw objections. Not only the moral tone of the piece, but the brutal behavior of the police in extracting a false confession from an innocent man were regarded as peculiarly American. The *Courier-Mail* described the play as dealing "with phases of life which happily have not developed here—phases which...arise from an excess of freedom—the liberty which unduly impinges on the liberty of others" (3 May 1910), while the *West Australian* assured its readers:

> Mr. Klein's plays...are distinctively American. We could not Anglicise *"The Lion and the Mouse"* by writing "House of Lords" for "Senate" or "London" for "New York." Still less could we represent Scotland Yard as practising that form of inquisition which is known in America as the "Third Degree."
>
> (23 July 1910)

Yet the same notice acknowledged the hold of the play on the audience, "Far more significant than the double call at the end of each act was the silence which prevailed while the story was being unfolded." The *Bulletin*'s Melbourne reviewer focused on the lesson to be learned:

> *The Third Degree*...professes to expose a scandalous misuse of power by persons in authority in the United States. The grains of truth in these awful indictments of foreign governments are worth thinking about. They have a local application. Australia has not yet had experience of a police system whereby blokes are worried into confessing crimes they didn't commit, but it knows of policemen who would work the system if they could.
>
> (1 September 1910)

Julius Knight was praised for his crusading attorney, Richard Brewster, while George Bryant was the bullying police detective, "cruel, vindictive, repellent" (*Argus*, 22 August 1910). As Annie, the wife of the accused, Katherine Grey again had the role of the woman battling alone against an overwhelming combination of money and political influence. While it was the same sort of role as that of

Shirley Rossmore, she was more highly praised for her craft. The *Advertiser* thought:

> She was vigorous without being hysterical, and in the most passionate scenes she acted with artistic restraint. She completely captivated the audience by the splendidly realistic fight she put up for her husband...Gesture, emphasis, expression, and action all fitted in admirably.

> (11 April 1910:3)

The *Argus* remarked that, "Her intense scenes rouse the house in enthusiastic manner many times, and in a way not often seen in a theatre nowadays" (22 August 1910).

It was Eugene Walter's *Paid in Full* that crossed the line for many. Because it is unpublished, a brief synopsis is necessary. Joe Brooks, an employee of a steamship company is so bitter and frustrated by his inability to provide for his wife, Emma, that he embezzles from his employer, Captain Williams. When the Captain catches on, Joe, knowing that the Captain is attracted to Emma, urges her to plead his case. The Captain appears willing to take advantage of the situation. He propositions her. When she refuses, he is delighted at her integrity and gives her a signed statement that her husband's accounts are in order. When Emma gives him the statement, Joe accuses her of infidelity. Indicting him for hypocrisy, she walks out.

Gerald Marr Thompson was offended, "The American author does not exercise the reticence of a great writer...like...Ibsen. For that reason it is necessary to warn... playgoers that...in its sexual aspect it is...outspoken" (*SMH*, 17 October 1910). In his scrapbook, he wrote that the play was, "Verging on the indecent."[3] He was not alone. The *Age* thought that "Clever analysis of character and occasional wit are little compensation for a sordid theme" (17 April 1911). Others, however, disagreed. While objecting to American "slang sayings...which are not understood by Australian audiences," the *Argus* thought the play "a commendable attempt to stem the tide of cheap sensational melodrama" (April 17 1911), while the *Advertiser* reported that "for intensity of dramatic situations and, withal, for a fine moral flavor, '*Paid in Full*' is all that can be desired" (29 May 1911).

While the Sydney Bulletin reporter thought that, "Miss Katherine Grey acts incomparably...one of those strong, helpful, and (above all) Good women...American men have worshipped" (20 October 1910), and the *Age* thought that, "Her playing...offered no false note" (17 April 1911), the Melbourne critic for the *Bulletin* concluded, "Here as elsewhere Miss Grey subdues too much—her people have something of the monotony of figures seen in a mist" (20 April 1911). George Bryant was praised as the Captain, and William Desmond was particularly liked for his portrayal of "Jimsy," a best friend to Emma and her husband.

If the sexual implications of *Paid in Full* troubled some, Edward Sheldon's *Salvation Nel* outraged all the Sydney dailies. They and their readers were shocked by the language and offended by the treatment of religion. The *Telegraph* noted, "Many...uttered distinct gasps of astonishment" (7 November 1910). The reaction insured that the play was not offered elsewhere. By contrast, Shaw's *Arms and the Man*, which played the same number of performances, was seen in every city. While the *Bulletin* disapproved of "the brisk pace of a knockabout farce" (3 March 1910), there was general agreement with the *Courier-Mail* that Katherine Grey was "refreshingly natural and femininely attractive" as Raina opposite Julius Knight (10 May 1910). She was also successful as Louka, the other young woman in the play, when she performed it with William Desmond. Apparently, both parts were amenable to the comic version of her persona of the lone woman fighting insurmountable odds.

William Desmond continued to act in Australia until the end of 1912. When Julius Knight returned to England, Williamson had brought him over to support Katherine Grey. After her departure the company's repertory was augmented by Conan Doyle's *The Speckled Band*, Paul Armstrong's *Alias Jimmy Valentine*, and William C. DeMille's *The Woman*, along with revivals of *The Silver King* and *The Sign of the Cross*. Reviewers compared Desmond unfavorably to Julius Knight. As the lawyer in *The Third Degree*, the *Telegraph* thought that "though his reading of the part displayed greater vigor than that of Mr. Julius Knight, it lacked the sedate weight and authority which his predecessor imparted. …A more definite air of reserve is demanded by the author" (5 December 1910). Similar criticism was voiced about his John Burkett Ryder, and he was frequently criticized for speaking too rapidly for the audience to understand: "He talks at the rate of about 400 words a minute" (*West Australian*, 17 July 1911). Everyone agreed that he was miscast as Sherlock Holmes: "His Yankee voice, Irish face, robust form and vigorous method ill accord with the familiar figure of Conan Doyle's tall, tired, cadaverous Englishman" (*Bulletin*, 5 October 1911:10).

It was in the title role of *Alias Jimmy Valentine* that Desmond won general approval. The *Argus* thought "Mr. William Desmond acted with an energy that drove the part home, carrying it over all incongruities" (26 February 1912). Based on O. Henry's story, "A Retrieved Reformation," the play tells the story of a safecracker who has reformed and taken a new identity after prison. He is forced to reveal himself in the presence of a police detective who is hunting him for an earlier crime, when a child becomes locked in a new bank vault for which a combination has not been set. Choosing to pick the lock and save the child, Jimmy is rewarded when the detective decides that the police claim on him is less powerful than the claim of his new life. The critics found the play's characters conventionally shallow, but they were intrigued as always by American police methods. In the final analysis, however, Desmond's energy, which some found to be natural, seemed purely theatrical to others, "Desmond's elocution, mannerisms, and make-up are equally unsuggestive of life beyond the stage" (*Bulletin*, 29 February 1912).

The last and most successful series of "crook" plays in Australia before the World War were those featuring Muriel Starr. She had begun acting in New York City during 1909, and her obituary stated correctly that "her great success took place during the first World War period in Australia" (*New York Times*, 20 April 1950, 29:1). Between May 1913 and September 1915, she appeared in all the cities except Hobart in a repertory of eight plays. Of the six emotional melodramas, she played Bayard Veiller's *Within the Law* throughout the period and nearly twice as often as George Broadhurst's *Bought and Paid For* or Alexander Bisson's *Madame X*. Three comic melodramas, *Under Cover* by Roi Cooper Megrue, *The Chorus Lady* by James Forbes, and *Nobody's Widow* by Avery Hopwood combined for almost as many performances as *Bought and Paid For*.

As in the case of Katherine Grey's repertory, Australian critics were careful to isolate the plays from Australian life. *Within the Law* was morally ambiguous. Falsely convicted of stealing from her employer and hounded by the police after her release from prison, Mary Turner is determined on revenge. Supporting herself and her associates by confidence schemes and extortion within the law, she marries the son of her former boss in order to extract a large payment for a divorce. When a police attempt to entrap her results, instead, in her husband being charged with murder, the situation is only saved by a pair of fortuitous confessions, one that clears him of murder and one that exonerates Mary from her original conviction.

Much of the play's interest comes from the behavior of police captain Burke, who rides roughshod over any legal restraints or moral niceties in his determination to punish those he thinks are criminals. Although Australians saw the American version, *Within the Law* had been popular in London in a British adaptation. The *Bulletin* thought the changes "foolish because the whole atmosphere is American. ...The policemen become caricatures when they are stated to come from Scotland Yard" (25 September 1913), and the *West Australian* observed that, "Its situations, characterisations, and developments...possess the charm of novelty for Australian audiences, to whom the conditions and possibilities of life, law, and police procedure in New York are something of a revelation" (18 May 1914).

Critical revulsion also quarantined subject matter from infecting the society. Reviews of *Bought and Paid For* stressed the "ugly" nature of its treatment of sex and marriage (*Herald and Telegraph*, 15 March 1915), while *Madame X* was characterized as "sordid and repulsive" (*Herald and Telegraph*, 6 July 1914). In the former, a wealthy man marries a shopgirl and supports her in luxury. However, when he drinks, he becomes sexually aggressive and brutal. He sees no reason to change because his business success has been the result of similar behavior. Only after she leaves him and lives in poverty does he reform. In the latter, a dying woman who has murdered her lover is found innocent because she had been abused as a wife years before.

There were few reservations, however, about Muriel Starr, her American colleagues, Charles Millward and Lincoln Plumer, or George Bryant. Indeed, the *Herald* noted that "anything will prove acceptable that is covered by the powerful art of stage favourites" (15 March 1915). In mock astonishment, the *Bulletin* cried, "Nobody plays to the gallery. These astonishing people don't seem to want to be interrupted by bursts of applause; they want to get on with business" (28 August 1913).

Starr was compared to both Katherine Grey and Margaret Anglin. In its review of *Within the Law*, the *Argus* described their common style at some length:

> For studies of shop-girls and stenographers, people who live by their work, and earn salaries sufficient to keep them alive and happy—or otherwise—the Americans surely have it all in their own hands. Miss Starr acts quietly, naturally. She flies into temper as an ordinary woman would, she snuffles quietly into a handkerchief as convincingly as any real girl who has lost a lover or done upon impulse a thing which calls for regret and for tears. Heroics!—there are none of them. Poses!—there are the natural poses of disdain and reflection and abandonment, all excellently studied. Her voice is like her acting, quiet and harmonious, level for the most part, but full of colour and expression where needed.
>
> (19 May 1913)

The *Bulletin* agreed. "She is not a Margaret Anglin. Miss Starr is less subtle, less artistic: and is therefore likely to be more popular. But, in her line of goods she is the best piece of goods we have seen out here since Margaret Anglin" (2 October 1913:8).

Her dominant persona was that of "the typical young woman that the average American playwright finds it impossible to do without. Very much alert, very keen witted and so clever as to be almost superhuman" (*Age*, 2 November 1914), with which the *Bulletin* agreed: "She is at her best in parts where a ready wit, a quick tongue and a large amount of self-reliance are wanted" (14 December 1914). While most notices found her voice quality agreeable, almost everyone thought that she spoke too rapidly and quietly, a problem compounded by American slang:

If Miss Starr would but speak a little slower and not turn her head away so much from the audience, her worthy efforts would be heard all the better, especially as it is necessary to follow the Americanese slang, which the programme has obligingly translated in some 60 instances.

(*Argus*, 14 December 1914)

As "O. K." noted, "People do speak up, as a rule, when excited" (*Bulletin*, 19 June 1913:30), and "Harrison O." obligingly transcribed examples: "We get from her hurried remarks like, 'OIforgotforgiveme,' and mutilated observations such as 'It's privige me so stinguish man'" (26 November 1914).

And although he reviewed her favorably, Gerald Marr Thompson noted that he and his wife "thought Miss Starr just a stock actress."[4]

The one role in which Muriel Starr seemed to vary her persona was that of Jacqueline in *Madame X*. It is the one role in which she was not young, energetic, and intelligent. The *West Australian* described her as a "haggard woman, whose beauty has gone, whose voice is hoarse and harsh…with solace only in drugs" (1 June 1914). The *Argus* critic thought that "Miss Muriel Starr showed herself a thoroughly accomplished actress in a difficult and thankless part. …It is not beautiful, it is not even pleasant, but it is art" (30 March 1914).

Starr's performance as Mary Turner became so familiar to Australian audiences that when Maggie Moore parodied it in the Christmas pantomime at Melbourne's King's Theatre, "The audience laughed until it drowned the last bitter wail" (*Argus*, 21 December 1914). Maggie Moore did not limit herself to parody of others in American crime melodrama. During 1914–1915 in Sydney and Melbourne, she played comic character roles in *Ready Money*, *The Argyle*

Case, and *Kick-In*. While none of the plays was particularly popular, Moore scored distinct success as a Negro cook in the first, and as an Irish boarding housekeeper in the third. By Christmas of 1915, however, Maggie Moore, Muriel Starr, and every other performer in Australia was competing with the World War for popular attention. The campaign at Gallipoli had ended, and the pages of the newspapers were filled with pictures and stories of dead and wounded Australian soldiers.

CHAPTER 13

The American Idiom: Comedy

ADDRESSING MEMBERS OF THE University of California's Philosophical Union in August of 1911, Harvard philosopher George Santayana noted that expansion and abundance had wiped out the sense of sin in America: "If you told the modern American that he is totally depraved, he would think you were joking, as he himself usually is. He is convinced that he always has been, and always will be, victorious and blameless."[1] Santayana's observation provides an insight into not only the nature of American humor, but also into its appeal to Australians.[2]

The American comic style is exemplified in *The Widow Bedott Papers* of Frances M. Whitcher, *The Biglow Papers* of James Russell Lowell, the fictions of Bret Harte and Mark Twain, and the newspaper columns of Artemus Ward and Mr. Dooley. It is a style of hyperbole that treats exaggeration and eccentricity as ordinary events. This contradiction manifests itself in both speech and action. Thus, the most outrageous lies and the most preposterous physical acts are told in a laconic manner epitomized by Twain's tale of the jumping frog. The characters in these tales are normally eccentric, and the longer the narrative, the more numerous and odd they become, because the interaction of eccentricities produces an increasing comic momentum, at the center of which is the comic protagonist, calmly assured of his own virtue and eventual triumph in the midst of the chaos that his behavior has created.

Many, perhaps most, educated Australians preferred the tradition of English humor in the works of W. S. Gilbert and Oscar Wilde as presented on stage by the London Comedy Company (1879), Mr. and Mrs. Robert Brough (1896–1906) and J. C. Williamson's Royal Comic Opera Company, but there was clearly an audience for the American style. Indeed, the humor in the stories by Henry Lawson and Joseph Furphy resembles the American more than the English, and the American influence is noticeable on nearly every page of *The Bulletin*. American stage comedy in Australia in the years before the First World War had four principal exponents: the comedies of Charles Hoyt, the companies of Nat Goodwin, William Collier, and Fred Niblo.

Charles Hoyt and Musical Farce

The first type of distinctive American humor to become popular was the musical farce. The practice of linking songs, dances, and other variety acts by means of a slender story first migrated from the United States to Australia with the Salsbury Troubadours between July 1877 and February 1878. Singing, dancing, and burlesquing other performers, they were entertaining if a trifle vigorous (*Town and Country Journal*, 28 July 1877). More elaborate examples of American musical burlesque in Australia included Edward Rice's *Evangelize* (1891), George Stephenson's *American Comedy Co.* (1903–1904), Kolb and Dill in vehicles originally created for Joe Weber and Lew Fields (1904), and the American Musical Burlesque Company featuring Burt LeBlanc (1913–1915).

While all these companies found audiences and gathered their share of sometimes grudging praise, the most successful exponents of what was on the way to becoming American musical comedy were the companies playing the works of Charles Hoyt. Two companies came from Hoyt's Theatre in New York City to Australia, one during the second half of 1896, the other for about the same period of 1899. Harry Conor was the leading man both times, but the second company featured the eccentric comedian and dancer Hugh Ward who became a resident of the Australian theatre.

A Trip to Chinatown was the most frequently performed of Hoyt's plays in Australia. Its plot consists of nothing more than a scheme by a group of young people assisted by a clever widow to evade the supervision of their elders in order to enjoy the night life of San Francisco's Chinatown. While the story is insignificant, the attitudes of its young characters is not. They set out deliberately to defy social convention. They see nothing wrong with that; they do not fear punishment; and they are utterly confident that they will succeed. They are perfect examples of the attitude described by Santayana.

The script was never intended as more than a vehicle for the abilities of the performers, and new jokes, songs, and dances were regularly introduced to attract repeat audiences. The company's performances were staged by Julian Mitchell (later stage director of Ziegfeld's Follies), and its general style of playing was described as vigorous but economical: "There is no waste. ...That is where the American style excels the English" (*Telegraph*, 29 June 1896), and notices in each city recorded crowded and enthusiastic audiences. The actors directed their performances to the audience and had no inhibitions about laughing at or applauding each other's efforts (*Australasian*, 26 September 1896; *Bulletin*, 24 June 1899).

Conor, a Hoyt specialist, was liked because he was never vulgar in his role as a well lubricated rake. He was described as "brisk in action, voluble in speech" (*Advertiser*, 10 September 1899), with "unbounded confidence in himself" (*West Australian*, 10 October 1899); moreover he "has the...advantage of being the only man in the co. who talks exactly like Mark Twain. The rest talk like somebody else—possibly Josh Billings" (*Bulletin*, 4 July 1896). Critics were charmed by the singing and dancing of soubrette Sadie MacDonald (who died of typhus, while the company was in Sydney), and astonished by the ability of dancer Bessie Clayton to kick above her head both in front and behind.

Hugh Ward remained in Australia with Williamson's comic opera company (1900–1903), playing such roles as the Bosu'n in *H. M. S. Pinafore*, the Sargeant of Police in *The Pirates of Penzance*, and the Duke of Plaza-Toro in *The Gondoliers*. After successful engagements in London, New York City, and elsewhere, he returned to Australia in the latter part of 1906 in a series of farces which exploited his ability to play roles requiring both agility and eccentricity. The *West Australian*'s description catches the essence of his typical character's appeal:

> Those who have seen Mr. Ward in similar characters will easily recall the roving eye which seems to search every corner of the room for a plausible evasion—the emphatic repetition of the charge against him as though this consti- tuted a complete exculpation—the twitch of the coat-tails, the mirthless laugh, and finally the 'explanation,' deliv- ered with a fine extemporaneous air (for the hundredth time perhaps).
>
> (31 May 1909)

In 1910 he became a partner in the management of J. C. Williamson, Ltd.

Nat Goodwin and Rural Melodrama

The most popular American comic actor other than Joseph Jefferson, Nat Goodwin described his sixteen weeks of playing in Australia from July to October 1896 as "disastrous."[3] Before coming to Australia, he had toured as Sir Lucius O'Trigger in Joseph Jefferson's star revival of *The Rivals*. He included this play in a repertory of established personal hits: *The Nominee* by William Yardley and Leander Richards, *A Gilded Fool* by Henry Guy Carlton, *In Mizzoura* by Augustus Thomas, and a piece which he premiered on the tour, *An American Citizen* by Madelaine Lucette Ryley.

In his autobiography, he blamed Williamson, with whom he had been friends for years, for ineffective advertising and personal rudeness. To make matters worse, Goodwin and his leading lady, Maxine Elliott, had both recently divorced their spouses, and their relationship to each other was the source of widespread speculation in the United States, which, Goodwin said, greatly upset her.[4]

While reporting that the small audiences were highly amused, critics felt that the American style of writing and playing was inferior to the British. As the *Age* put it, "Of the purely boisterous humor that is physical, that comes from a quaintness or absurdity of expression, and an extravagance of action, there is an abundance" (27 July 1896). Goodwin presented the conventional comic persona of the quick-witted opportunist. No matter what accidents or unintended consequences occur, he always turns certain disaster into improbable triumph. In *The Rivals*, in which Goodwin took Jefferson's part as Bob Acres, he presented the awkward, gentle, kindly rube. Goodwin extended the Acres persona in the rural comic melodrama *In Mizzoura*, which was his most often performed and most unreservedly praised performance.

Around the turn of the century, an urbanizing United States looked nostalgically at life on the vanishing family farm, which joined the mining camp and cowboy frontiers as demi-Edens in which natural virtue flourished. Australian audiences never saw the greatest hits in this sub-genre of sensation melodrama, *The Old Homestead* by Denman Thompson and *Shore Acres* by James A. Herne, but American actor Robert McWade revived *Rip Van Winkle* in Melbourne and Sydney (1889–1890), and there were Sydney productions of Neil Burgess's *The County Fair* (1891–1892), Charles Dazey's *In Old Kentucky* (1895), and Joseph Arthur's *Blue Jeans* (1898). Most successful of all was the American company that played Ann Crawford Flexner's *Mrs. Wiggs of the Cabbage Patch* in 1908.

The rural melodrama, like its frontier predecessors, showed that it was sometimes necessary to ignore both law and social custom in order to do good—a sentiment frequently expressed in Australian popular culture. This was the context for Goodwin's artistic success as Jim Radburn, the Sheriff of Bowling Green, Pike County, Missouri. Jim is standing for the Democratic nomination (equivalent to election) to the state legislature, but he loves Kate, daughter of his opponent for the office. Because she is college-educated, Kate cannot see Jim's virtues (even though he secretly financed her education). She prefers a citified stranger. When the stranger turns out to be a train robber, Jim lets him go to spare Kate's feelings. His action is revealed when the robber is killed in another town, but the citizens forgive Jim because of his motive. He remains sheriff, Kate's dad having won the nomination, and it seems clear at the end of the play that Kate has figured out where her romantic interest lies. Thus, in a rural community, a well-intentioned, essentially selfless person can manage to reconcile love and law, charity and justice, something that seemed increasingly hard to do in the city. The *Advertiser*'s comment is typical:

> What Bret Harte has done for the mining camp...Augus-
> tus Thomas has done for the backwoods village. ...One
> cannot but feel a sense of unwonted exhilaration in
> watching...a glimpse of that life...which is only to be
> found in the remote and sparsely populated districts of
> America...Jim Redburn...is one of nature's gentlemen.
>
> (31 August 1896)

Not only was the play praised for its virtue and truth-fulness, but all the actors were deemed natural and unaffected, qualities they had not always seemed to possess in the other plays. Goodwin was unanimously praised for his restraint, for his ability to suggest emotion without overtly expressing it, and the *Bulletin* reviewer made the obvious comparison to Jefferson (8 August 1896). In one sense, perhaps the best review was unpublished. Gerald Marr Thompson, the *Herald*'s chief critic assigned a colleague to write the published reviews of Goodwin's company, but in his scrapbook he recorded that *In Mizzoura* "simply delighted us. I have only had three or four evenings as nice in my whole career."[5]

William Collier and Farce Comedy

While the *Dramatic Mirror* thought him "probably the best light low comedian in this country" (13 February 1901), Willie Collier had neither the reputation nor the range of Nat Goodwin. He specialized in Hoyt farces before becoming a star in his own right. He was always the urban opportunist whose natural goodness eventually overcame any short-sighted considerations of personal gain, but he lacked Goodwin's gentle charity. Nevertheless, he and Goodwin shared a style of playing. The Australian papers compared both men's acting to that of Daniel Frawley in its restraint and in its lack of direct appeal to the audience.

The circumstances of his appearance offer an insight into Williamson's operating connections. According to the *Herald*, Williamson had secured the Australian rights for *On the Quiet* by Augustus Thomas and *The Dictator* by Richard Harding Davis in 1904, but American manager Charles Frohman wanted to present them in London with Collier as the star. Since Frohman was the most important American producer of first-class comedy and drama in the United States, with theatres in both New York City and London, and since he was by then Williamson's most important source for plays and productions, the Australian manager agreed to wait (4 March 1905).

Williamson would have had reason to be more confident of Collier's success than of Goodwin's because Collier's type of performance had already proved wildly popular in Australia in the work of English actor Charles Arnold. Arnold had first toured Australia in *Charley's Aunt* during 1900, and he returned in 1901 with three farces by American playwright George Broadhurst: *What Happened to Jones*, *Why Smith Left Home*, and *The Wrong Mr. Wright*. The jokes in this genre depend on the relationship between identity and respectability. Finding themselves in compromising situations, characters not only assume others' identities, but attribute their own to others. They are always in danger of discovery, the consequences of which will be some combination of social, financial, and romantic ruin. Invariably, however, the truth is revealed in the light of extenuating circumstances that restore and usually enhance their positions.

Collier's company was a close-knit group that had been together for three years. In addition to the star's sister, Helen, it included Jefferson's nephew, Charles Jefferson Jackson, along with John Barrymore, and Mabel Tallieferro. During their brief Australian tour (26 May to 3 August 1906) confined to Melbourne and Sydney, Collier played a wise-cracking, feckless charmer on a high wire without a net. Reviewing *The Dictator*, the *Age* reported that:

> The whole performance...was one procession of good, honest, wholesome fun, without a single suggestive interlude, and both play and players were most manifestly to the taste of the crowded audience which laughed itself almost to a state of physical exhaustion before the final curtain.
>
> (28 May 1906)

While the *Herald* praised Collier's restraint—"We recollect no one who so consistently declines to over-elaborate his points for the sake of an extra laugh" (28 July 1906)— other reviews make it clear that both plays were full of physical action:

> Falling over furniture, stampeding about the deck of a yacht, flying through doorways or out of windows, indulging in cakewalks round a breakfast table, and conducting themselves throughout with an amazing amount of high pressure energy.
>
> (*Age*, 18 June 1906)

Yet they failed in much the same manner Goodwin had ten years earlier. Although the *Bulletin* thought "Willie Collier and co. in *The Dictator* were just the brightest thing in farcical comedy that Melbourne and Sydney have jointly and severally refused to take kindly to," they ascribed the failure to circumstances:

> Collier and co. had been accustomed to playing in small houses, where every inflection of a low-pitched voice was duly effective. At Her Majesty's (Melb.), where the luckless Australian tour started, Collier nearly busted his vocal organ in the attempt to speak up. ...*The Dictator* provided an astonishing object-lesson in the risks of theatrical speculation. It opened to a great Saturday night

house, and the press criticisms were a chorus of praise, but the Monday night audience was a record in slumps. The drop from the first-night takings to the second night's takings—the stream of gold diminished to a trickle—is about the saddest of the J. C. Williamson firm's recollections.

(3 June 1909)

Fred Niblo

Fred Niblo and his wife, Josephine Cohan, were not the last comedians from America to visit Australia before the First World War (they were followed by the comic actor Sheppard Camp and by a company playing the urban immigrant comedy *Potash and Perlmutter*), but they were the last to succeed in a big way. Playing precisely the same kind of humor as William Collier, they were nearly as popular as J. C. Williamson and Maggie Moore had been. Primarily vaudeville performers (he was a monologist while she was an acrobatic dancer and singer, as well as the sister of George M. Cohan), they hadn't performed together until the season of 1911–1912, when they headed the Western combination of Winchell Smith's *The Fortune Hunter*. Shortly afterwards, they brought it and several other farces to Australia and New Zealand from August of 1912 to December 1914. When Josephine Cohan returned to the United States in poor health at Christmas, Niblo replaced her with Australian actress Enid Bennett. After Josephine Cohan died, Niblo married Bennett. They returned to America where he became a movie director and producer while she acted in films.

Of the seven plays in Niblo's repertory, *The Fortune Hunter* was most often performed, but George M. Cohan's three plays (*Get-Rich-Quick-Wallingford*, *Seven Keys to Baldpate*, and *Broadway Jones*) together accounted for nearly half of all the performances. Winchell Smith had already proved a popular author in Australia. His *Brewster's Millions* had played over a hundred performances in 1908 during a tour of all the major cities by Williamson's Royal Dramatic Company starring Thomas Kingston and featuring Mrs. Robert Brough, and while George M. Cohan's works were new to Australian audiences, they were conceived in the same genre as those presented by Nat Goodwin and William Collier. Thus the success of Niblo's company may have depended as much upon audiences finally being familiar enough with the style as it did on the performers' mastery of the style.

All the critics commented on the similarities of plot and character in *Wallingford*, *Broadway Jones*, *Fortune Hunter*, and James Forbes's *The Traveling Salesman*: A young man of dubious character moves from the city to a small town where he earns wealth and love by means of hard work and sharp dealing. The *Herald* explained that "To an American audience the spectacle of a man struggling to make money by dubious means may be supremely interesting, because the making of money is there the chief business in life" (4 November 1912), and the *Bulletin* observed, "The…audiences…are mainly masculine. Getting rich quick is a masculine job. That is why there are not female bookies" (10 October 1912). Of the other plays, two (*Excuse Me* by Rupert Hughes and *Officer 666* by Augustin McHugh) were typical Broadhurst-style farces, while Cohan's *Seven Keys to Baldpate* was hailed for its unique blend of farce and murder mystery.

All critics were equally clear about the swiftly paced casual style of the players. Comparisons with Collier were common, there were occasional comments about the need for the actors to speak up, and there were the usual complaints about unfamiliar slang and customs: "American comedy is not as a general thing popular in Australia—

perhaps because our people are not 'to the manner born' for appreciation of the jerkiness and velocity which are usually such pronounced features" (*West Australian*, 28 November 1913), but the *Advertiser*'s summary was more typical:

> Tempestuous and hilarious. ...The piquant accent of the people of the great Republic, with their picturesque phrases and expletives, was abundantly in evidence, while by gesture, dress, and method of shaving the quaint personages...were cleverly differentiated.
>
> (3 November 1913)

Niblo was generally praised. However, when the *Bulletin* wrote that, "Niblo is one of the finest and most finished actors we have had here" (7 May 1914:8), it was rebuked by "O.K." in *Poverty Point*: "He has rushed the public into accepting the same sort of quick-tongued American as four or five different characters" (18 June 1914). Josephine Cohan was liked for her delicacy and reserve, but Niblo was the show.

The company was further bolstered by Harry Corson Clarke, an experienced performer of farce, and by George Bryant in various heavy roles. Niblo made several films of his plays for J. C. Williamson, Ltd., and footage from *Officer 666* survives. While the playing strikes the modern viewer as broad (in the manner of all silent film), it also possesses the physical precision of timing and execution characteristic of the film comedy of Mack Sennett and Charles Chaplin.

Part of Niblo's success may have been because as Australians found themselves drawn into the European war, the springs of British comedy seemed to dry up. Niblo and his repertory represented a qualitatively distinctive American alternative:

It is to America that we are turning more and more...for the realistic farce. ...American playwrights have rediscovered the beauties of mock seriousness which passed with Sir William Gilbert...Mr. Niblo [understands] the method. ...What an admirable Bunthorne or Ko Ko, or Sir Joseph Porter he would make.

(*Argus*, 18 May 1914)

While the whole of Europe is in ferment, and the bloodiest battles of history are being fought...it is almost a matter of necessity to go to America.

(*Age*, 26 April 1915)

However reluctantly, Australians once more used representations of and from America as an element in continuing to construct their own national identity.

Observations

AUSTRALIAN NOVELIST AND POET David Malouf has characterized the American experience as a "shadow history to be
reflected or avoided" that has been present in Australia
from the beginning, but he believes that the defining quality
of the Australian character is the permanent tension
between a culture inherited from the northern hemisphere
and the physical environment of the southern hemisphere.[1]
Perhaps the history of American plays and players on the
Australian stage during the nineteenth century captures
something of Australian efforts to adjust that tension.
Although located in the northern hemisphere, the climate,
geography, plants, and animals of North America vary
greatly from those of Europe, especially as one moves west.
The scale and variety of the landscape, the profusion of
species, and the abundance of mineral riches combine to
create a sense of place and society that would be more
familiar to an Australian than would the confines of
Europe.

Despite distance and the rigors of travel in the nineteenth century, Australians saw as representative a sample
of the available plays and players as any Anglo-European
provincial audience. Among the great actors who dominated their respective national stages, they saw Bernhardt and
Duse in the fullness of their artistry. While Henry Irving
was frequently promised but never came, Ellen Terry
appeared at the end of her career to give a series of readings, rather like a ghost of her former self. They saw Edwin

Booth when he was an apprentice, and they nurtured Joseph Jefferson just as his genius blossomed. They saw many stars of lesser magnitude: Gustavus Vaughn Brooke, Barry Sullivan, and Mrs. Scott-Siddons from Great Britain; Mr. and Mrs. Stark, Josephine Gougenheim, William E. Sheridan, Nance O'Neil, Margaret Anglin, William Collier, Nat Goodwin, and Fred Niblo from the United States. As a theatrical province, Australia also had resident actors of similar status: Alfred Dampier, George Darrell, Bland Holt, George Rignold, Mr. and Mrs. Robert Brough, J. C. Williamson and Maggie Moore. They also saw many Americans who had starring ambitions: Mary Provost, William H. Leake, Louise Pomeroy, Janet Waldorf, Cora Potter, Minnie Tittell Brune, Katherine Grey, and Muriel Starr, several of whom achieved their greatest success in Australia.

The same may be said for plays. The traditional repertory centered on the plays of Shakespeare was as often performed in Australia's cities as in those of America and Great Britain. Australians saw nearly all the principal melodramas, farces, and comedies of the day, as well as a fair sample of both British and American variety entertainment. The relative success or failure of any particular play or player, then, cannot be reasonably attributed to lack of choice or understanding. It can only be attributed to local taste, to the way in which it did or did not fit into Australian culture.

Australians and Americans shared certain experiences that set them apart from Great Britain. Both cultures began with a small group of British emigrants settling in a wilderness inhabited by indigenous people whom they did not understand. Moreover, the political and economic development of both societies had depended on a continuing stream of additional settlers from Europe spreading out to the west of the continent, discovering and exploiting its natural resources. The British knew little of pioneering frontier settlements and hostile natives until the second half of the nineteenth century, and even then, their experience in India, Africa, and the Malay states was different from that of Americans and Australians because they were always a tiny minority compared to the indigenous population.

Although an extension of a country with a long history of control by a small, land-owning aristocracy, Australia was more egalitarian than Great Britain. There were never more than a handful of members of aristocratic families in the colonies. The overwhelming majority of Australians were wage-earning laborers and tradesmen, with a small middle class of entrepreneurs and professionals. On a day-to-day basis, they were much like Americans in their economic and political ideas, which may be why the great Australian novelist of the end of the nineteenth century, Joseph Furphy, chose an American as the spokesman for his ideas in that part of his epic published as *Rigby's Romance*.

For all their similarities, Australia and America differed in certain important ways. First, Australians were free immigrants. Even convicts had been free-born and could achieve freedom again, whereas the United States had long supported slavery. Second, Americans had rebelled against the home country, and violence and civil war were a major part of their history. Third, America was able to support a large population, and both individuals and groups could amass enough wealth and power to control the nation. Fourth, America guaranteed certain individual rights by law.

Reviewing the careers of these plays and players, it seems clear that Australians used images or representations of the United States as a variable in the creation of their own culture. While the cultural ideal changed over time, America and Americans were always the foil to the British. Most frequently, American plays and players were used as scapegoats. They represented qualities that Australians thought they should disapprove of. Not infrequently, this disapproval took the form of denying an apparent similarity between Australian and American culture, as in frontier and urban crime melodramas. Similarly, American performers were criticized when their stage behavior departed too much from the Australian norm of respectability. However, reviewers often articulated a different standard than the audience, disapproving of some plays and players who were manifestly successful, while approving of some that failed.

However it was used, the image of America and of Americans remained reasonably consistent on the Australian stage and provides Americans with an image (a face reflected in the window) of how they looked to others.[2] Americans seemed almost anarchically individualistic. They were willing to disregard or violate not only social convention but also the law to achieve their goals. Thus, they were prone to far greater and more frequent violence than seemed acceptable. All Americans seemed to live by Davey Crockett's motto, "Be sure you're right, then go ahead." While this meant that both characters and actors were often crude or vulgar compared to the British, they were also more energetic and pragmatic.

Americans seemed obsessed with money and wealth because they derived their personal identity from how they made their money, and they derived their social identity from how much of it they made. They were willing to do anything, sacrifice anything, to get richer, not only for material comfort but for social status.

Generally, Australians disapproved of or were uncomfortable with these qualities. Australians had a greater sense of an obligation to share with and support others in their community, even at the expense of personal gain, than they thought Americans did. Two factors seem to lie at the heart of the Australian value of "mateship." The first is the loyalty that convicts felt toward each other in the face of a repressive military hierarchy. The second, which extended convict loyalty long after transportation ceased, was the difficulty of survival in a harsh environment. Compared to Britain, Australia is a vast territory, and, compared to both Britain and the United States, it has a harsh climate. In the outback free Australians practiced the same loyalty to each other as the convicts had. It was a matter of survival dictated by conditions over which they had little control.

There were cultural areas, however, in which Australians came to share America's individualism and violence. In matters of race, they had more in common with Americans than they did with the British. While the British exploited indigenous people, they abolished slavery and the slave trade in their domain, and they had no non-European indigenous population to deal with in Great Britain itself. By contrast, white Australians had an aboriginal population, and they were also afraid of being overrun by immigrants or conquerors from Asia. For these reasons, their attitudes toward non-Europeans resembled those of the United States more than those of Great Britain. They treated their aboriginal population in much the same manner as Americans treated their natives, and they shared the American fear and loathing of Asians.

Finally, in matters of gender, their attitudes paralleled those of the Americans as they approached the twentieth century. The ideal of the Victorian middle class was that the woman managed the domestic side of life as the angel in the house, while the man managed affairs in the great world outside. In the lexicon of Victorian women, the siren and the fallen women were opposites of the angel. The former sought to destroy domestic tranquility by seducing the man, while the latter had betrayed her domestic trust for the sake of passion. If such women repented, they could be forgiven, but they could never be allowed to enter the domestic circle again.

In general, Americans took a more liberal view of gender roles, particularly in the frontier setting. The siren or fallen woman was often a savior, and the frontier contributed its own unique term to the Victorian lexicon in the person of the free-spirited, unmarried girl. In some sense, obviously the descendent of the soubrette, the character of the girl challenged the fundamental assumption of the Victorian gender scheme that all women were meant to be controlled by a man. The girl ignored or defied such control unapologetically. Although she might love a man and even marry him, she didn't need him. Her economic, social, and moral survival were in her own capable hands.

The attitude embodied in this character may account for the relatively greater success of actresses from America in Australia, compared to their male counterparts. By definition, the actress defied the Victorian gender scheme. Even if married and a loyal wife and good mother, she earned her living outside the home, and she did so by displaying herself for money to a largely male audience. This parallel to prostitution, along with the often adjacent premises of their work, has been frequently remarked, but there may be other factors in play as well.[3]

The female star or leading actress was as much of a free and independent agent as her male opposite. It may be that American actresses were thus seen as signs of American individualism as much as they were seen as signs of anything else, and, to the extent that they appeared in the role of the girl, American plays could have reinforced this reading of their performance. Thus, it is possible that the American actress signified something to her audience that crossed over normal gender boundaries. Not only did the American girl appeal to Australians because they recognized equivalent characters in their own society, but also because they recognized equivalent aspirations of their own for freedom and independence, regardless of gender.

When I look at Australia through the window of the history of theatrical performance, my own shadowy image gazes back. That is because we see ourselves in the differences of others. This view confronts us with our energy, our inventiveness, and our willingness to abandon convention. It also confronts us with our greed, violence, and corruption. While Australians could pick and choose from among these qualities, we cannot. We are what we see reflected.

References to daily newspapers are given in the text according to the following abbreviations.

Advertiser	*Australian Advertiser*, Adelaide
Age	*The Age*, Melbourne
Alta	*The Alta California*, San Francisco
Argus	*The Argus*, Melbourne
Australasian	*The Australasian*, Melbourne
Bulletin	*Bulletin*, Sydney
Courier	*Courier Mail*, Brisbane
DM	*Dramatic Mirror*, New York
Mercury	*Hobart Mercury*, Hobart
SMH	*Morning Herald*, Sydney
Telegraph	*The Daily Telegraph*, Sydney
WA	*West Australian*, Perth

Notes

INTRODUCTION

1. Roland Barthes, *Mythologies*, trans. Stephen Heath (NY: Hill and Wang, 1972), 128–145. For the practical use of public myth, see William H. McNeill, "The Care and Repair of Public Myth," *Foreign Affairs* 61 (Fall 1982), 1–13.

2. Regis Debray, *Transmitting Culture*, trans. Eric Rauth (NY: Columbia University Press, 2000).

3. Robert C. Allen, *Horrible Prettiness: Burlesque and American Culture* (Chapel Hill, NC: University of North Carolina Press, 1991), 34–38.

4. Isaiah Berlin, "Historical Inevitability," in *The Proper Study of Mankind: An Anthology of Essays* (New York: Farrar, Straus and Giroux, 1997), 119–190.

5. Simon Schama, *Landscape and Memory* (New York: Harper Collins, 1995), 134.

CHAPTER 1

1. For those unfamiliar with Australian history, the most complete source is Geoffrey Bolton, ed., *The Oxford History of Australia*, 5 vols. (Melbourne: Oxford University Press, 1986–1992). I also recommend Geoffrey Blainey, *A Shorter History of Australia* (Sydney: Vintage Books, 2000), Stuart Macintyre, *A Concise History of Australia* (Cambridge, UK: Cambridge University Press), and Richard White, *Inventing Australia: Images and Identity 1688–1980* (St. Leonard's, New South Wales: Allen and Unwin, 1994).

2. Russell Ward, *The Australian Legend* (Melbourne: Oxford University Press, 1958), 15.

3. Charles Darwin, *The Voyage of the Beagle* (Garden City, NY: Anchor Books, 1962), 431–443.

4. Ward, 16–17.

5. Beverly Kingston. *Glad, Confidant Morning, The Oxford History of Australia, 1860–1900* (Oxford, UK: Oxford University Press, 1988), 175.

6. My account of the rise of the middle class is taken from Charles Moraze, *The Triumph of the Middle Classes* (New York: World Publishing, 1966).

7. Moraze, 359.

8. See, for example, Sarah Stickney, *The Women of England, Their Social Duties, and Domestic Habits* (New York: B. Appleton, 1839).

9. C. Hartley Grattan, *The United States and the Southwest Pacific* (Cambridge, MA: Harvard University Press, 1961), 1–103.

10. Frances Trollope, *Domestic Manners of the Americans* (New York: Dodd, Mead, 1832).

11. Charles Dickens, *American Notes and Pictures from Italy* (Oxford, UK: Oxford University Press, 1957), 244.

12. Charles Dickens, *Martin Chuzzlewit* (Oxford, UK: Oxford University Press, 1957), 273.

13. Ibid., 237.

14. Roger Bell, "The American Influence," in Neville Meaney, ed., *Under New Heavens: Cultural Transmission and the Making of Australia* (Melbourne: Heinemann, 1989), 327.

15. For the Australian experience in the American gold rush, see Jay Monaghan, *Australians and the Gold Rush: California and Down Under, 1849–1854* (Berkeley, CA: University of California Press, 1966).

16. For the American experience in the Australian gold rush, see L. G. Churchward, *Australia and America, 1788–1972: An Alternative History* (Sydney: Alternative Publishing Cooperative, 1979); and Daniel E. Potts and Annette Potts, *Young America and Australian Gold: Americans and the Gold Rush of the 1850s* (St. Lucia, Queensland: University of Queensland Press, 1974).

17. For the voyage of the Shenandoah, see Tom Chaffin, *Sea of Gray: The Around-the-World Odyssey of the Confederate Raider Shenandoah* (New York: Hill and Wang, 2006). For its Australian episode, see Cyril Pearl, *Rebel Down Under: When "Shenandoah" Shook Melbourne, 1865* (Melbourne: William Heineman, 1970).

18. The best survey of Australian theatre is Harold Love, ed., *The Australian Stage: A Documentary History* (Sydney: New South Wales University Press, 1984). Additional information can be found in Katharine Brisbane, *Entertaining Australia* (Sydney: Currency Press, 1991), and Philip Parsons, ed., *Companion to Theatre in Australia* (Sydney: Currency Press, 1995).

19. For a good analysis of the social function of melodrama, see Elaine Hadley, *Melodramatic Tactics: Theatricalized Dissent in the English Marketplace, 1800–1885* (Stanford, CA: Stanford University Press, 1995).

20. Michael Booth, *Theatre in the Victorian Age* (Cambridge, UK: Cambridge University Press, 1991), 134.

21. For the concepts of absorption and reflection, see Michael Fried, *Absorption and Theatricality* (Berkeley, CA: University of California Press, 1980).

22. For a good analysis of acting style and its changes, see Joseph Donohue, "Actors and Acting," in Kerry Powell, ed., *The Cambridge Companion to Victorian and Edwardian Theatre* (Cambridge, UK: Cambridge University Press, 2003), 17–35.

23. Kingston, 174.

24. George Vandenhoff, *The Art of Elocution As An Essential Part of Rhetoric With Instruction in Gesture and an Appendix of Oratorical, Poetical, and Dramatic Extracts* (London: Sampson Low, 1867), 167.

25. Frederick Marryat, quoted in Kingston, 183–184.

26. T. S. Eliot, "Tradition and the Individual Talent," Frank Kermode, ed., *Selected Prose of T. S. Eliot* (London: Faber and Faber, 1975), 38.

CHAPTER 2

1. For background on California theatre during this period, the best source remains George R. MacMinn, *Theater of the Golden Era in California* (Caldwell, ID: The Caxton Printers, 1941). The best source on Mr. and Mrs. Stark is a monograph in Lawrence Estavan, ed., *San Francisco Theatre Research Monographs*, vol. 3 (San Francisco: Works Progress Administration, 1938).

2. Eric Irvin, *Dictionary of the Australian Theatre*, 1788–1914 (Sydney: Hale and Iremonger, 1985), 169–170.

3. Charles Vernard Hume, *The Sacramento Theatre, 1849–1885* (diss., Stanford University, 1955), 53–69.

4. George C. D. Odell, *Annals of the New York Stage* (New York: Columbia University Press, 1927–1949), vol. 5.

5. Hume, 71–74.

6. Hume, 85–86.

7. Humphrey Hall and Alfred J. Cripps, *The Romance of the Sydney Stage* (Sydney: Currency Press, 1996).

8. It was reported that Kate Denin turned down an offer from Melbourne manager George Coppin for a year's contract (*DM*, 16 February, 1907).

9. For a full account see Eric Irvin, "Laura Keene and Edwin Booth in Australia," *Theatre Notebook* 23:3 (Spring 1969): 95–100.

10. For an account of Buchanan's career, see my article, "McKean Buchanan, the Actor as Character," *Theatre Studies* 24/25 (1977/78–1978/79): 95–106.

11. Mark Twain, *The Adventures of Huckleberry Finn* in *Mark Twain: The Mississippi Writings* (New York: Library of America, 1982), 758.

CHAPTER 3

1. Harold Love, James Edward Neild: *Victorian Virtuoso* (Melbourne: Melbourne University Press), 54.

2. Odell, Vol. 5:362. Further biographical information on Mary Provost was published in the *New York Clipper* (10 May 1856).

3. James Smith Papers, MSS 212, Mitchell Library, State Library of New South Wales, Sydney.

4. Walter M. Leman, *Memories of an Old Actor* (San Francisco: A. Roman 1886), 284.

5. This and all of the following correspondence is in James Smith Papers.

6. Bronwyn Mason, *Negotiating the Pacific: George Coppin's Business Transactions With California, 1864–1881* (diss., University of New South Wales, Sydney, 1999), 302.

CHAPTER 4

1. Hazel Waters, "That Astonishing Clever Child: Performers and Prodegies in the Early and Mid-Victorian Theatre", *Theatre Notebook*, 50:2 (1996): 78–94.

2. Unidentified clipping reprinting a review from *London Era* of 1857 in J. M. Forde scrapbook, "The Stage," Q792/N, Mitchell Library, State Library of New South Wales, Sydney, vol. 185:23.

3. Hall and Cripps, 228.

4. J. M. Forde, "Mummer Memoirs" by "Hayseed," *Sydney Sportsman* (31 May 1905) in J. M. Forde newspaper cuttings, Q792.099/F, Mitchell Library, State Library of New South Wales, Sydney, vol. 23A:93.

5. Hall and Cripps, 241.

6. Anthony Trollope, *Australia*, 2 vols. (New York: Hippocrene Books, 1987), I: 177.

CHAPTER 5

1. Nils Erik Ekvist, *Caricatures of Americans On the English Stage Prior To 1870* (Port Washington, NY: Kennikat Press, 1951).

2. William R. Taylor, *Cavalier and Yankee: The Old South and American National Character* (New York: Harper, 1961).

3. For a comprehensive survey of minstrelsy and *Uncle Tom's Cabin* in Great Britain, see Sarah Meer, *Uncle Tom Mania: Slavery, Minstrelsy and Transatlantic Culture in the 1850s* (Athens, GA: University of Georgia Press, 2005). The most provocative analyses of the social function of blackface are W. T. Lhamon, Jr., *Raising Cain: Blackface Performance From Jim Crow To Hip Hop* (Cambridge, MA: Harvard University Press, 1998); and Eric Lott, *Love and Theft: Blackface Minstrelsy and the American Working Class* (New York: Oxford Univeristy Press, 1993).

4. Enkvist, 112–113.

5. N. W. Senior, *American Slavery* (London: Longmans, 1856), 38–39.

6. Bruce McConachie, "Out of the Kitchen and Into the Marketplace: Normalizing Uncle Tom's Cabin for the Antebellum Stage", *The Journal of American Drama and Theatre*, 3:1 (Winter 1991): 5–28.

7. Beverley Kingston, *Glad Confident Morning, The Oxford History of Australia, 1860–1900* (Melbourne: Oxford University Press, 1988), 163–167; Jan Kociumbas, Possessions, 1770–1860, *Oxford History of Australia* (Melbourne: Oxford University Press, 1992), 150–177.

8. Russell Ward, *The Australian Legend* (Melbourne: Oxford University Press, 1958), 130.

9. Potts; Ward, 130–132; Richard Waterhouse, *From Minstrel Show To Vaudeville: The Australian Popular Stage, 1788–1914* (Kensington, New South Wales: University of New South Wales Press, 1990), 145–151.

10. See the studies by Sarah Meer and Richard Waterhouse.

11. The most comprehensive account of Jefferson's life is by Arthur Bloom, *Joseph Jefferson: Dean of the American Theatre* (Savannah, GA: Frederick C. Beil, 2000), while Benjamin McArthur offers superb analysis, *The Man Who Was Rip Van Winkle* (New Haven, CT: Yale University Press, 2007). I have supplemented Richard Waterhouse's account of Hosea Easton's life.

12. Jefferson's views on acting are contained in Chapter 16 of *The Autobiography of Joseph Jefferson*, ed. Alan Downer (Cambridge, MA: Harvard University Press, 1964), and in Otis Skinner, *Footlights and Spotlights, Recollections of My Life on Stage* (Indianapolis, IN: Bobbs Merrill), 253–254.

13. Easton's autobiographical press release was printed in the *West Australian*, 17 August 1896. For the first Hosea Easton, see George R. Price and James Brewer Steward, eds., *To Heal the Scourge of Prejudice: The Life and Writings of Hosea Easton* (Amherst, MA: University of Massachusetts Press, 1999).

14. Ike Simond, *Old Slack's Reminiscence and Pocket History of the Colored Profession from 1865 to 1891* (Bowling Green, Ohio: Bowling Green University Popular Press, 1974).

15. For the history of Hicks and his companies, see Robert Toll, *Blacking Up: The Minstrel Show in Nineteenth-Century America* (New York: Oxford University Press, 1974), 203; and Richard Waterhouse, 56–57.

16. See Russell Ward, *The Australian Legend*, 224; Daniel and Annette Potts, *Young America*, and Richard Waterhouse, 145–151.

17. Waterhouse, 93.

18. For an account of Jack Johnson in Australia, see Randy Roberts, *Papa Jack: Jack Johnson and the Era of White Hopes* (New York: Free Press, 1983), 55–67.

CHAPTER 6

1. For San Francisco variety theatres, see Edmund M. Gagey, *The San Francisco Stage, a History* (Westport, CT: Greenwood Press, 1950), 72–73. For DeAngelis, see Jefferson DeAngelis and Alvin F. Harlow, *A Vagabond Trouper* (New York: Harcourt, 1931), 18, 33.

2. Clay M. Greene, "My Seventy Five Years Off and On," unexpurgated copy with editorial changes, typed ms., 2 vols., Special Collections, Oradre Library, University of Santa Clara, 69–70. For corroborative data, see William R. James, "Clay Meredith Greene (1852–1933): A Case Study of an American Journeyman Playwright" (diss., University of Iowa, 1969).

3. Ian Dicker, *J. C. W.: A Short Biography of James Cassius Williamson* (Sydney: Elizabeth Tudor Press, 1974), 39–43.

4. Maggie Moore, "Account of Her Tours," AM 145, Mitchell Library, State Library of New South Wales, Sydney. The only reliable published account of Maggie Moore's life is her entry in *The Australian Dictionary of Biography* (Melbourne: Cambridge University Press, 1966).

5. Dicker, 51.

6. Dicker, 66.

7. Dicker, 66–68.

8. Dicker, 90–95.

9. W. H. Ford, *Theatrical Reminiscences*, ms. B966, Mitchell Library, State Library of New South Wales, 18–19.

10. This summary is based on an ms. copy of the play in the J. C. Williamson Collection, Australian National Library, Canberra. Its relationship to what Williamson and Moore actually performed is a matter of conjecture.

CHAPTER 7

1. Kingston, 108.

2. Geoffrey Blainey, *The Tyranny of Distance: How Distance Shaped Australia's History*, rev. ed. (Sydney: Pan Mcmillan, 1967), 169.

3. Manning Clark, *A Short History of Australia*, 3d ed., rev. (New York: Penguin, 1987), 63–64.

4. Kingston, 32.

5. Clark, 163.

6. Russell Ward, 209–210.

7. Blainey, 222, 267–268.

8. Kingston, 9–11.

9. Kingston, 43–51; Clark, 169–170.

10. Blainey, *A Shorter History of Australia*, 122–124.

11. Samuel Hynes, *The Edwardian Turn of Mind* (Princeton, NJ: Princeton University Press, 1968); Barbara Tuchman, *The Proud Tower* (New York: Macmillan, 1966).

12. Kingston, 97–98, 147, 282; Geoffrey Serle, *The Rush To Be Rich: A History of the Colony of Victoria, 1883–1889* (Melbourne: Melbourne University Press, 1971), 91; Robert Gollan, "The Australian Impact," in *Edward Bellamy Abroad*, ed. Sylvia Bowman (New York: Twayne, 1962), 119–136.

13. R. E. N. Twopeny, *Town Life in Australia* (London: Elliot Stock, 1883; Sydney: Sydney University Press, 1973), 90.

14. Twopeny, 111, 119.

15. The best summaries of the new Australian nationalism are Russell Ward's and Geoffrey Serle's *From Deserts the Prophets Come: The Creative Spirit in Australia, 1788–1972* (Melbourne: Heinemann, 1973).

16. L. G. Churchward, 73–74.

17. F. A. McKenzie, *The American Invaders* (London: Grant Richards, 1902; New York: Arno Press, 1976), 222.

18. James Bryce, *The American Commonwealth*, 3d., ed., 2 vols. (London: Macmillan, 1908), 2:282–283.

19. Tuchman, 13.

20. Kevin J. Phillips, *The Cousins' Wars: Religion, Poolitics and the Triumph of Anglo-America* (New York: Basic Books, 2000).

21. Mark Twain, *Following the Equator: A Journey Around the World*, (Hartford, CT: American Publishing Co., 1897); Mirriam Shillingsburg, *At Home Abroad: Mark Twain in Australia* (Jackson, MS: University of Mississippi Press, 1988).

CHAPTER 8

1. Frederick Marker and Lise-Lone Marker, "Actors and Their Repertory" in Michael R. Booth et al., *The Revels History of Drama in English, 1750–1880, Volume 6* (London: Methuen, 1975): 121–141.

2. George Bernard Shaw, "The Old Acting and the New," in *Plays and Players: Essays on the Theatre* (London: Oxford University Press, 1952), 52–54.

3. Harold Love, *James Edward Neild, Victorian Virtuoso*, 211–224.

4. Janette Gordon-Clark, "From Leading Lady to Female Star: Women and Shakespeare, 1855–88," in John Golder and Richard Madelaine, eds., *O Brave New World: Two Centuries of Shakespeare on the Australian Stage* (Sydney: Currency Press, 2001), 72–86.

5. For descriptions of American styles of acting, see Garff B. Wilson, *A History of American Acting* (Bloomington, IN: Indiana University Press, 1966) and James E. Murdoch, *The Stage; or, Recollections of Actors and Acting* (Philadelphia: J. E. Stoddart, 1880).

6. For the middle class and their values, see Peter Gay, *The Bourgeois Experience, Victoria to Freud, 5 Vols.* (New York: Oxford University Press, 1984–1998).

7. Martin Meisel, *Realizations: Narrative, Pictorial, and Theatrical Arts in Nineteenth-Century England* (Princeton, NJ: Princeton University Press, 1983), 4–81.

8. Stephen C. Schultz, "Toward an Irvingesque Theory of Shakespearean Acting," *Quarterly Journal of Speech* 61 (December 1975): 428–438.

9. Margaret Williams, *Australia on the Popular Stage, 1829-1929: An Historical Entertainment in Six Acts* (Melbourne: Oxford

University Press, 1983), 220–230; Vivien Gardner and Susan Rutherford, eds., *The New Woman and Her Sisters: Feminism and Theatre, 1850–1914* (Ann Arbor, MI: University of Michigan Press, 1992).

10. Barbara Welter, *Dimity Convictions: The American Woman in the Nineteenth Century* (Athens, OH: Ohio University Press, 1976), especially "The Cult of True Womanhood," 21–41.

11. For a description of this style, see Charles Shattuck, *Shakespeare on the American Stage from Booth and Barrett to Sothern and Marlowe* (Washington, D. C.: Folger Library, 1987), 65–70.

12. Gerald Marr Thompson, Annotated scrapbooks of clippings, 1886–1934, 14 vols. Mitchell Library, State Library of New South Wales, 1901–1905:129.

13. John LeVay, *Margaret Anglin, A Stage Life* (Toronto: Simon and Pierre, 1989), 9.

14. George Du Maurier, *Trilby* (London, Penguin Books, 1994), 33. L. Edward Purcell, "Trilby and Trilby-Mania, the Beginning of the Bestseller System, Journal of Popular Culture, 11:1 (Summer 1977): 62–76.

15. Shattuck,103–111.

16. Eric Irvin, *Dictionary of the Australian Theatre, 1788-1914* (Sydney: Hale and Iremonger, 1985). For Miln's earlier career, see Alan Woods, "Quality Wasn't Expected: The Classical Tours of George C. Miln," *Theatre Studies* 24/25 (1977/78–1978/79): 139–147.

CHAPTER 9

1. Cora Potter, "The Age of Innocence and I," *Hearst's International Cosmoplitan* 94 (March-May 1933), April: 49.

2. Julie Mills, "Harold Kyrle Money Bellew," *Australian Dictionary of Biography, 1891–1939* (Melbourne: Melbourne University Press, 1979): 7:259–260.

3. Potter, May, 76.

4. *Evening Transcript*, New York, 6 March 1886; Potter, March, 149.

5. Shattuck: 120-25; Nym Crynkle, *DM*, 12 and 19 January 1889.

6. Nellie Stewart, *My Life's Story* (Sydney: J. Sands, 1923), 83–84.

7. For a comparison of Bernhardt and Cora Potter, see Corille Fraser, *Come to Dazzle, Sarah Bernhardt's Australian Tour* (Strawberry Hills, NSW: Currency Press, 1998).

8. The careers of Rankin and O'Neil are meticulously detailed by David Beasley, *McKee Rankin and the Heyday of the American Theater* (Waterloo, Ontario, Canada: Wilfrid Laurier University Press, 2002).

9. Gerald Marr Thompson, 1897–1900:177–178.

10. "enjoyed immensely," Gerald Marr Thompson, 1897–1900:225.

11. J. P. Wearing, *The London Stage, 1900-1909: A Calendar of Plays and Players* (Metucheen, NJ: Scarecrow Press, 1981) 182-184.

12. I have traced Tittell Brune's early career through San Francisco and Portland, Oregon, daily newspapers, the *Dramatic Mirror*, San Francisco city directories and other material in the California Historical Society, San Francisco.

13. Frederick Warde's autobiography describes his season with Tittell Brune, *Fifty Years of Make-Believe* (New York: International Press Syndicate, 1920). For Espy Williams and *Unorna*, see Paul T. Nolan, "The Life and Death of a Louisiana Play: *Espy Williams' Unorna, Louisiana History*, 5.2 (1964): 143–159. Tittell Brune's American tours can be traced in the *Dramatic Mirror*.

14. Gerald Marr Thompson, 1901–1905:342.

15. Gerald Marr Thompson, 1901–1905:350.

16. For a full account of the production and its reception, see Veronica Kelly, "J. C. Williamson Produces Parsifal, or the Redemption of Kundry: Wagnerism, Religion, and Sexuality," *Theatre History Studies* 15 (June 1995): 161–181.

17. Gerald Marr Thompson 1905–1909:222.

CHAPTER 10

1. For George Darrell, see Eric Irvin, *Gentleman George, King of Melodrama* (St. Lucia, Queensland: University of Queensland Press, 1980); the text of *The Sunny South* has been edited by Margaret Williams (Paddington, New South Wales: Currency Press, 1975). For Dampier and Walch, see Margaret Williams, *Australia on the Popular Stage*; the text of *Robbery Under Arms* has been edited by Richard Fotheringham (Paddington, New South Wales: Currency Press, 1985).

2. Bronwyn Mason, 239–242.

3. R. B. Harwell, "Civil War Theatre: The Richmond Stage," *Civil War History 1* (1955): 295–304; "Brief Candle: The Confederate Theatre," *Proceedings of the American Antiquarian Society* 81 (1971): 41–160.

4. Letter of 1 July 1904, Gerald Marr Thompson,1905, endpaper; Gerald Marr Thompson 1901–1905:135–136.

5. Jane W. Stedman, "From Dame to Woman: W. S. Gilbert and Theatrical Transvestism" in *Martha Vicinius, A Widening Sphere: Changing Roles of Victorian Women* (Bloomington, IN: Indiana University Press, 1977): 20–37.

6. Odell, 13:16–17.

7. Twopeny, 86.

8. Odell, 12:17–18.

CHAPTER 11

1. Letter from Sydney, 28 September 1902, *The Papers of Will Rogers*, ed. Arthur Frank Wertheim and Barbara Blair (Norman, OK: University of Oklahoma Press,), I: 449–450.

2. The classic exposition of this culture is Richard Slotkin, *Gunfighter Nation: The Myth of the Frontier in Twentieth Century America* (New York: Atheneum, 1992).

3. The best biography of Theodore Roosevelt is H. W. Brands, *T. R., the Last Romantic* (New York: Basic Books, 1997).

4. *Ranch Life and the Hunting Trail: The Works of Theodore Roosevelt, National Edition* (New York: Charles Scribner's Sons, 1926), 1:269–459. For scholarly elaboration, see Robert G. Athearn, *The Mythic West in Twentieth-Century America* (Lawrence, KS: University of Kansas Press, 1986); Richard Hofstadter, *The Age of Reform* (New York: Knopf, 1955); and G. Edward White, *The Eastern Establishment and the Western Experience* (New Haven, CT: Yale University Press, 1968).

5. Irvin, *Gentleman George*, 63; Margaret Williams, 173–180.

6. For the Wild West Show, see Don Russell, *The Lives and Legends of Buffalo Bill* (Norman, OK: University of Oklahoma Press, 1960); Sarah J. Blackstone, *Buckskins, Bullets, and Business: A History of Buffalo Bill's Wild West* (Westport, CT: Greenwood Press, 1986); and Dexter Fellows and Andrew A. Freeman, *This Way To the Big Show* (New York: Halcyon House, 1936).

7. Nate Salsbury, "The Origins of the Wild West Show," *Colorado Magazine* 32 (1955): 205–211.

8. MS B 752, Mitchell Library, State Library of New South Wales, Sydney.

9. For a full account of the Passion Play, see Alan Walter Nielson, *The Great Victorian Sacrilege: Preachers, Politics, and the Passion, 1879–1884* (Jefferson, NC: McFarland, 1991).

10. Augustus Thomas, *Arizona: A Drama in Four Acts* (New York: R. H. Russell, 1899), 124.

11. Williams, 217–230.

CHAPTER 12

1. For a thorough analysis of this period see Richard Hofstadter, *Age of Reform.*

2. For an analysis of this sub-genre, see Lynn Marian Thomson, "The Crook Play," *Journal of American Drama and Theatre* 13:1 (Winter 2001): 1–35.

3. Gerald Marr Thompson, 1909–1913:84.

4. Gerald Marr Thompson, 1913–1918:104.

CHAPTER 13

1. George Santayana, *The Genteel Tradition in American Philosophy* (Berkeley, CA: University of California Press, nd), 7.

2. For a stimulating discussion of the appeal of humor, see Ted Cohen, *Jokes: Philosophical Thoughts on Joking Matters* (Chicago, IL: University of Illinois Press, 1999), 28.

3. Nat Goodwin, *Nat Goodwin's Book* (Boston, MA: 1914), 173.

4. Goodwin, 233–239.

5. Gerald Marr Thompson 1895–1897:65.

OBSERVATIONS

1. David Malouf, *A Spirit of Play: The Making of Australian Consciousness* (Sydney, New South Wales: ABC Books, 1998)

2. For a contemporary American explanation of the following qualities, see his 1910 address to the American Historical Association, "Social Forces in American History," in Frederick Jackson Turner, *The Frontier in American History* (New York: Henry Holt, 1920), 320-321.

3. For a full discussion of this topic see Tracy C. Davis, *Actresses as Working Women: Their Social Identity in Victorian Culture* (London: Routledge, 1991).

Index of People, Places and Topics

Index of Plays and Productions

www.ingramcontent.com/pod-product-compliance
Lightning Source LLC
Chambersburg PA
CBHW071212090426
42736CB00014B/2787